CAMPUS CONFIDENTIAL

CAMPUS
CONFIDENTIAL

100 startling things you don't know about Canadian universities

Ken S. Coates
Bill Morrison

James Lorimer & Company Ltd., Publishers
Toronto

James Lorimer & Company Ltd., Publishers acknowledges the support of the Ontario Arts Council. We acknowledge the financial support of the Government of Canada through the Canada Book Fund for our publishing activities. We acknowledge the support of the Canada Council for the Arts which last year invested $20.1 million in writing and publishing throughout Canada. We acknowledge the Government of Ontario through the Ontario Media Development Corporation's Ontario Book Initiative.

Library and Archives Canada Cataloguing in Publication

Coates, Kenneth, 1956–
    Campus confidential : 100 startling things you don't know about Canadian universities / Ken S. Coates, Bill Morrison.—2nd ed.

Includes bibliographical references.
Also issued in electronic format.
ISBN 978-1-4594-0435-9

    1. Universities and colleges—Canada. 2. Education, Higher—Canada.
I. Morrison, William R. (William Robert), 1942– II. Title.

LB2329.8.C2C63 2013   378.71   C2012-908082-9

James Lorimer & Company Ltd., Publishers
317 Adelaide Street West, Suite 1002
Toronto, ON, Canada
M5V 1P9
www.lorimer.ca

Printed and bound in Canada
Manufactured by Friesens Corporation

For our grandchildren:
William Griffin, Spencer Griffin, Victoria Griffin, Katie Coates,
Christopher Coates, Hazel Coates.
Graeme Gibbons, Ella Gibbons, James Tosoff, Henry Tosoff,
Quinn Morrison, John Morrison.
In the hope that the universities that await them will be up to the
challenges of the twenty-first century.

Contents

VI. A Professor's Life 149

VII. Universities in Canadian Society 179

Introduction to the Second Edition

The publication in 2011 of the first edition of *Campus Confidential* coincided with the beginning of a long-needed national debate about the nature and future of universities in Canada. To a degree that we have never seen before, commentary about universities has flooded the Canadian media—newspaper columns, talk shows, radio, and television. The Quebec students' strike in the summer of 2012 was a major national story. The reason for all this interest is simple: parents are worried about their children's career prospects and how families will cope with rising costs. Recent graduates are struggling with an unfriendly work environment, with many having to take low-end, unskilled jobs to pay the bills. Governments and employers want more attention paid to the needs of a changing workforce. Taxpayers wonder if they are getting value for their money. A final reason for this new interest is simply the percentage of the population going to university. Decades ago, when it was less than 5 per cent, it was a minority concern. Now almost a third of the population is at university (and counting the colleges, close to half are taking some form of post-secondary education). With university boosters claiming that soon three-quarters of new jobs will require a degree, it's become everybody's business. This interest is all relatively recent: before *Maclean's* began its rankings in 1980, there was virtually no public discussion of the strengths and weaknesses of Canadian universities.

Perhaps surprisingly—and this itself is telling—this debate has not been raging on university campuses. With the notable exception of those in Quebec, the universities themselves have been largely immune to the national angst about the future of post-secondary education. Students, faculty members, and administrations have not been eager to engage with the growing discussion about the purpose and function of universities. In sharp contrast to the more provocative and edgy commentary in the *American Chronicle of Higher Education*, the pages of *University Affairs*,

Canada's leading magazine devoted to post-secondary education, include only occasional articles on the critiques and shortcomings of the system.

The silence, indeed, has been deafening. Students outside Quebec have been surprisingly quiet about rising tuition fees and mounting debt loads; student radicalism in most of the country is largely a spent force. Faculty members have only complained quietly about growing class sizes and increased pressure to secure competitive grants and publish scholarly works. University administrators have been forthright in their complacency, citing doubtful arguments about the economic value of a university degree, asking for more money to pursue their "excellence agendas," recruiting ever more students, and making only minor steps toward institutional reform. The Government of Ontario's brief proposal on changes to Ontario's universities has given only shallow treatment to a system desperately needing a serious re-evaluation. And one of the most thoughtful commentaries in years on the Canadian university system, *Academic Transformation: The Forces Reshaping Higher Education in Ontario* by Ian Clark, Greg Moran, Michael Skolnik, and David Trick, has received depressingly little public attention.

It's not going to be easy to deal with the challenges facing Canada's post-secondary system. There is no national post-secondary education system; instead, we have thirteen provincial and territorial approaches, combined with a national commitment to basic research. Though government still pays more than half the cost of operating them, Canadian universities are relying less and less on provincial government grants to pay the bills. Accordingly, they are also ensuring that governments are not dictating institutional policies and priorities. Not surprisingly, as the universities have insisted upon having substantial independence from them, the provincial governments have responded by offering vague directions and fiddling with budgetary requests.

What we have, then, is stalemate. To a degree that is still unknown, the Canadian public appears to want substantial changes in the university system. They want more access, better-quality instruction, improved job prospects for graduates, more-supportive campus environments, more government regulation, and a more practical orientation to university programming. There are demands for smaller class sizes, more student-faculty engagement, and lower fees. But the students still come in record numbers, graduate school enrolments grow, parents fork over money for ever-increasing tuition fees, students take on more debt, governments continue to pay for new buildings, programs, and activities, and Canadian academics continue to receive some of the highest faculty salaries in the world. People's demands on the system, and therefore the ideas for change, are contradictory and inconsistent. Canadians want more universities, and better universities, at less cost to themselves and to government. Faculty and university administrators want more money, less teaching, more research funding, and greater autonomy. This is hardly a recipe for national consensus.

There is, of course, Quebec. For more than half of 2012, Quebec students poured onto the streets by the tens of thousands. They effectively stopped post-secondary education in the province for a full semester. At first they just wanted a small tuition hike rolled back. But these protests morphed into more complicated demands for everything from completely free tuition, to student input into university budgets, to a more general critique of capitalist society. The students played a significant role in toppling the Liberal government of Jean Charest. The Parti Québécois minority government, elected in September 2012, paid its debts as a matter of top priority, rolling back the planned tuition hikes and continuing with a proposed summit on post-secondary education that would allow students to influence university budgets. While public opinion polls made it clear that the majority of Quebecers opposed the students' demands and had no objection to higher tuition fees (which were still by far the lowest in the country), the PQ and its student supporters were not to be denied.

Scarcely a week goes by now without someone shining a new light on the Canadian university system. The *Globe and Mail* ran a long investigative reporting series on the troubles facing universities in the country. *Maclean's* continues its annual ranking of Canadian institutions and works to sustain discussion about universities. Through 2012, an extensive debate raged about the economic value of a university degree, with critics (including us) questioning the universities' often-touted "promise" of a $1.3 million advantage in lifetime income for a Bachelor's degree over a high school diploma.

We wrote *Campus Confidential* because we thought that

Canadians—students, parents, members of the general public, faculty, and administrators—deserved to have an open discussion about the strengths and weaknesses of the Canadian system. To be clear, there are impressive strengths in Canada's universities, at least twenty-three of which rank among the world's top five hundred institutions. But there are weaknesses, too, particularly on such questions as admission standards, the number of young people who go to university (or think they should), the undergraduate student experience, and the transition from university study to the workplace. *Campus Confidential* was warmly received, we were delighted to discover, by university faculty as much as by parents and students. Our academic colleagues love universities as much as we do, and many of them are eager to see the system improved. They worry, too, about the career prospects for their students and about over-crowded classrooms and students who work too much to pay their tuition and living expenses. The book touched a nerve, one that was even more sensitive than we had initially believed.

This revised edition of *Campus Confidential* includes twenty-six new chapters, reflecting suggestions and ideas that arose out of our conversations with Canadians about the first book, and updates and changes to many of the other chapters. We have dropped a number of chapters that seem, in retrospect, to have been less meaningful to readers, and have added others that addressed repeated questions or ideas. We have kept the tone and intent of the book intact, for we know that Canada needs a passionate and informed debate about the future of the nation's post-secondary institutions. There are some contradictions, since we view some issues from more than one side. We disagree with each other on two matters—university athletics and compulsory core courses—and the chapters reflect this disagreement. As before, this book is fuelled by our deep commitment to the ideal and the practice of universities in Canada. After ninety years in universities between us, we are proud of its strengths and accomplishments. Like many of our colleagues, as well as students, parents, governments, and others, we worry about the shortcomings of the system and the lethargy of universities in responding to changing times. Canada's universities are impressive places. But they can and should be even better.

We could have ended this introduction with that hopeful observation, but we have a more ominous thought on which to close. If university presidents were to put their ears to the ground, they might hear a distant rumbling; the sound of the Canadian public shifting its attention to universities, and not in a friendly way. It is too soon to predict revolution. There is, so far, no evidence that the system is keen on reforming itself; perhaps the inertia and resistance to change in the system will beat back any public desire for substantial changes to the multi-billion dollar Canadian university system. But people are becoming increasingly unhappy with the system: unhappy with rising costs, rising debt, crowded classes, dismal job prospects on graduation, and, perhaps most of all, with the increasing pressure to send their children, and everyone else's children, to university so that they won't fall as losers by the economic wayside. Those who love the system would be wise to join the revolution lest it occur without them.

Introduction to the First Edition

Universities are supposed to provide answers to the big questions in life—but they have generated many questions of their own. Does our university system work? Are employers happy with the graduates? Why might some universities have to close? Are students well served by their teachers and institutions, and do they work hard at their studies? Does academic research really fuel national prosperity? Do universities give good value for money? (They cost vast sums to operate. The current operating budget of the University of Toronto is $1.6 billion—more than that of the province of Prince Edward Island.)

Who really pays for the cost of an undergraduate education? How are Canadian universities doing by international standards? Why are there so many universities, and should students really be studying on-line? What do faculty members do in the summer, and are their salaries reasonable? Why are low university tuition rates one of the major financial benefits given to wealthy Canadians? Are corporations driving academic agendas at Canadian universities?

These and dozens of other questions have troubled us for years. We have wondered why there was not more discussion about these issues, which should matter to people well beyond the campus boundaries.

Universities play an important, but largely unexamined, role in our communities and our country. Academics don't like it when outsiders critique their operations, but since universities operate on public money they are not, and should not be, free from scrutiny and criticism. Some of it can be pretty nasty: the now-defunct *Frank* magazine used to publish a column called "The Groves of Academe," which poked cruel fun at the foibles of academics, and there is much anxiety on campus when the *Globe and Mail's* Margaret Wente turns her witty but acerbic pen to matters scholarly. In United States bookstores, there are shelves full of volumes decrying the absurdities and failings of universities and colleges.

Canadians, in contrast, are much more quiet, polite, and calm about discussing their university system—perhaps too much so. *Campus Confidential* is intended to be provocative and informative. We want Canadians to think deeply about the nature of the university and the choices we must make in the coming years about the system's future. Consider this book a conversation starter.

We do not hate universities and this is not an exposé. Rather, we care deeply about them. We don't come to praise higher education, nor to bury it, but to suggest ways it can be improved. Canadian universities are not in crisis—yet. But we do think there are some major and worrying forces at play. We'd like to see the system prepare for them instead of being blindsided by them. We believe we have one of the best university systems in the world, but we also think it could be made a good deal better.

Next to health care, education is the largest sector of our economy, and universities consume a large percentage of the education spending. Despite this, people know surprisingly little about how universities actually work. This isn't a pitch for huge new infusions of public money either. We argue that the money in the system could be spent more intelligently and to greater effect.

We hate to hear the phrase "it's only academic." It suggests we spend our time in esoteric and irrelevant pursuits. We decided to write a practical, not an "ivory tower" book. We wanted to get straight to the point, without providing masses of examples and piles of evidence—as academics properly and expertly do most of the time. We offer observations and ideas derived from many years of studying and working in universities. The hundred short chapters that make up this book deal with issues vital to young people thinking about university, to students already in university, to faculty coping with increasing demands on their time and abilities, to administrators trying to achieve the best results on a limited budget, and to the general public wondering what goes on behind the greenery on those ivy-covered walls—in short, to just about everybody.

We are a disparate pair. One of us was born in Ontario, the other in Alberta. Bill started university in 1959, spent all but two of the following fifty-one years as student, teacher, and administrator, and retired, as Professor Emeritus, in 2010. Ken started his studies in 1974 and, save for one year in Japan and one in Vancouver, has been in the system continuously since then. We've studied and worked at the following institutions as teachers and administrators: McMaster, Western Ontario, Toronto, Queen's, British Columbia, Manitoba, Brandon, Victoria, Northern British Columbia, Lakehead, Quest, New Brunswick (Saint John), Saskatchewan, and Waterloo in Canada, Waikato in New Zealand, and Florida State and Duke in the United States. It sounds rather as if we can't hold down a job, but remember that this list covers nearly ninety years between the two of us!

We have engaged in discussions over the years with many of our colleagues and professional friends about the shape and nature of our university system, and asked some of them to review this book for mistakes and oversights, but the ideas (and the errors) remain ours. We particularly want to thank Kelley Teahen, Rick Miner, James Barnett, Ernie Barber, Bill Chesney, Mark Evered, Sean Van Koughnett, Bud Walker, James Skidmore, Tobi Day-Hamilton, Feridun Hamdullahpur, Tim Kenyon, David Docherty, Tara Collington, Greg Poelzer, Emanuel Carvalho, Robert W. Park, Bruce Muirhead, Lynne Jelokhani-Niaraki, Paul Doherty, Dave Hannah, Michael Atkinson, Kelly Saretsky, Meg Beckel, Chris Read, Clive Keen, Keith Taylor, John Goyder, Diane Young, and Paul Munroe.

Universities are enormously important to the economic and social health of Canada. If the country is to continue to prosper throughout the lives of our children and grandchildren, universities have to prosper too, although perhaps not in their current form. Canada needs an open and aggressive debate about the role and purpose of universities, about the activities of students and faculty, and about the multi-billion dollar expenditures made with the firm—but largely uncontested—assumption that this investment will make Canada better and more prosperous. The ideas in *Campus Confidential* have been bubbling for a long time, and we know that many Canadians want to know a great deal more about universities. We hope you find this book a good place to start.

Ken S. Coates, BA, MA, PhD, Johnson-Shoyama Graduate School of Public Policy, University of Saskatchewan
Bill Morrison, BA, MA, PhD, DLit (Hon.), Professor Emeritus of History, University of Northern British Columbia

I

A Student's Guide to University

 # University Isn't for Everyone

So you want to go to university. Good for you. For thousands of Canadians, it's a fine choice. As you think about it, though; let us offer you a few words of friendly advice.

First, ask yourself this question: why do you want to go? Is it because your parents want you to, because you are really interested in what university has to offer, because your friends are going, because you can't think of anything else to do, because you want the secure career that a university degree promises, because the idea of learning about the world fascinates you, because you'd like to learn a skill that you could use to help humankind? All of the above? None of them?

It's important to know why you are going. Not everyone who starts university finishes it. At some places the drop-out rate approaches 50 per cent—nearly half the people who start, don't get a degree. Some quit, some flunk, others go elsewhere. Sometimes it's because they find it too difficult, and other times they decide it's not for them. The drop-out rate is much lower in professional programs, and overall, nationally, it's about 15 per cent, or one in seven.

Ask yourself another question: do I like to read? Not Harlequin Romances or *The Da Vinci Code*, but books about the world. Do you read a newspaper, either in print or on-line? Are you interested in politics, the Hubble Space Telescope, foreign countries, Shakespeare, the Large Hadron Collider, the Roman Empire? That's what university is about. If you are rolling your eyes, well…

Do you have the necessary skills? It can be hard to tell. High school grades are no longer a reliable indication. You may have graduated with 75 per cent, which was a very good result two generations ago, but nowadays it won't get you into a prestigious place. The median at McGill for incoming students in 2009 was 90 or 92 per cent, depending on the province you came from. There are plenty of places that will take you at 75 per cent or less, but you may have to relocate.

Is there something you'd rather do first? Travel perhaps, join the workforce, or do volunteer work? It won't hurt to wait a year or two—the universities will still be there, and you'll have a better idea of what you want. Don't wait too long, though.

Would you rather work in a field that doesn't require a degree? Perhaps the skilled trades? You can make just as much money, start making it earlier, do what you really want to do—not what someone else thinks you should do—by going to a technical institution.

If you decide not to go right away, or ever, you've not necessarily made a bad choice. University isn't for everyone. If, on the other hand, you decide that it's for you, then you have our best wishes. Good luck!

2 Should Tuition Be Free?

In the spring and summer of 2012, the province of Quebec was convulsed by a series of student protests that began when the provincial government announced that university fees in the province would rise by $325 a year over the next five years. The government apparently thought that this rise would not be controversial, since Quebec had the lowest fees in Canada by a considerable margin and, even after the hike, which would leave Quebec's tuition fees at $3,000 by 2016, they would still be significantly lower than those at universities in neighbouring Ontario (which were already $6,100 in 2012). Lucky Quebecers, to pay less than half the fees of their neighbours, right? If you thought so, you weren't listening to the Coalition large de l'Association pour une solidarité syndicale (CLASSE), which launched a series of protests and marches in the streets on Montreal and elsewhere. There were sympathy protests and sit-ins in other provinces too, but they didn't amount to much.

Everyone knows what happened next. The protests seriously disrupted classes at the French-language universities, and they went on all summer. The provincial government of Jean Charest tried to negotiate, and then passed a rather draconian law making the protests illegal. When none of this worked, Charest called an election, which resulted in a weak minority government led by Pauline Marois and the Parti Québécois. Almost the first thing that Marois did after taking office was to cancel the increase. Without breaking stride, CLASSE began to agitate to have all fees abolished, and for tuition to be free.

Apart from the internal provincial politics involved in the issue, the interesting question behind the episode is this: why should or shouldn't post-secondary education be free for students? The CLASSE manifesto of July 2102 (English translation) speaks to this point, but it talks more about the strike as a springboard for further social action—"the problem of tuition fees opened the door to a much deeper malaise," and so on. The document does, however, make this argument:

> Free access does more than simply banish prices: it tears down the economic barriers to what we hold most dear. Free access removes the stumbling-blocks to the full flowering of our status as humans. Where there is free access, we share payment for shared services...Where is justice, when a hospital can charge a lawyer the exact same fee as a bag clerk? For the lawyer, the amount is minimal; for the bag clerk, it is a back-breaking burden.

So the argument is that (a) university fees limit people's ability to develop fully as humans; (b) if everyone benefits, then everyone pays, presumably through taxes; and (c) fees weigh more heavily on people who are economically disadvantaged—a grocery clerk is less able to afford them than a lawyer.

The point about flowering is not made in the French original, and is really a social rather than an economic question: Can people reach their full potential as humans without a university degree? One would hope so. The real case for free tuition rests on the other two points: university education, like primary and secondary education, is good for society as a whole as well as for individuals; and fees discriminate against low-income people.

The answer to the last argument is not free tuition, which benefits the rich, too, but a generous system of bursaries for people of limited economic means who have the potential to benefit from university. Let the children of wealthy families pay full fees (and higher taxes), and support the children of the poor. What's unjust about that? You might argue that such a scheme would make the poor dependent on the charity of the rich, but that's no more true of bursaries than of any social benefit—such as the Old Age Assistance plan.

The question really hinges on whether you consider post-secondary education to be a private rather than a social benefit, such as primary and secondary education clearly are—having young people literate and numerate, and thus employable, benefits everyone. Certainly the education of a medical doctor benefits society—we need doctors—though of course doctors make a good living from their services. But suppose a student wants to take something that is of less obvious benefit to society: suppose she wants to take an (imaginary) Bachelor of Mime Studies, because she has always longed to fulfill herself as a mime. Is there a general social benefit here? Does society need mimes? Is this something taxpayers should support for four years? It's pretty clearly a private rather than a social benefit. And what of the third of Quebec university students who fail to complete a degree? How does supporting them benefit society? Perhaps we could adopt the Estonian model (see chapter 16) and subsidize degree programs that society clearly needs—but this seems unlikely to be acceptable in Canada; certainly it's not what the Quebec students want.

Quebec has the lowest university fees in Canada, and it also has the highest university drop-out rate in the country. And Quebec's admission standards are just as low as they are everywhere else. A system that easy to get into is bound to attract many people who are unsuited to be in it, and the cheaper it is, the more unsuitable people it's likely to attract. What a waste of money and of human potential.

Consider the Skilled Trades

Doug installs high-end kitchens for a living, and he is doing very well. He's smart, talented, and very good at running his own company. By all measures, his is a classic example of the fulfilling careers available to those in the skilled trades.

Doug also has a university degree. He went to university because his parents expected it, many of his friends were going, and his high school teachers pointed him in that direction. He loved working with his hands and had a strong mix of entrepreneurship, creativity, and technical proficiency. But he bought the university propaganda and came under the spell of the counsellor's mantra: go to university, get a degree, aspire to a white-collar career.

He slogged through his BA degree, doing as little as possible to get a C– average. He never really warmed to his academic discipline, though he did party a lot. He worked with a carpenter in his spare time and in the summer to pay the bills and clearly loved this work more than book learning. He graduated because he was expected to, but he had no interest in pursuing a career related to his studies.

Doug shows up statistically as a university success story. Universities would claim that his studies gave him a greater appreciation of the world and even made him more successful at his chosen trades and business career. You could also argue that university was a waste of money for both him and the government and that he should have been given more encouragement to consider a trades career from the beginning. Doug viewed university as an extension of high school, as something smart kids were just expected to do. He bears no grudge against the university he attended—he had fun there out of class—but he doesn't see the place as critical to his subsequent success.

Mark is a somewhat different case. He was an academic superstar in high school, with stratospheric grades in math and science. He had his choice of the best universities in Canada and received big scholarships. He completed his MSc and then his PhD at a prestigious institution. He married a fellow scientist and seemed destined for a fine scholarly career. But the passion was gone. He no longer found pleasure in scientific discovery and realized he did not want to be an academic. Now in his late twenties, he had no plans for what to do next, and he had no other marketable skills.

Then Mark, like Doug, discovered he loved working with his hands and had a gift for woodwork. With no regrets, he stepped away from the academy and began a career making high-quality furniture.

Doug and Mark's experience, and that of thousands like them, shows that universities are not for everyone, not even for every intelligent young person. The idea that people with brains must get degrees—and that people with no degrees have no brains—is appallingly wrong and unfair.

The lesson here is that the trades should be given equal billing with university education in high school. Students should be encouraged to follow their passions, capitalize on their abilities, and find a career that brings satisfaction—and a decent income. Universities are too often presented as the best—if not the only—option for bright students. This is bad for the students, and for the economic health of Canada.

University Tuition Is a Bargain

Is a university education a private good, a public one, or a combination of the two? Is it a solid investment in students' futures; or is it an investment by the state, designed to increase the nation's productivity, competitiveness, and general well-being, and therefore a shared or common good? If it's the first, it seems fair that students (and their parents) should pay the lion's share of the cost of a university education. If it's the second, then the state and taxpayers should pay much of the cost. Which is it?

This question is a matter of endless debate, with governments and universities raising fees as much as they dare, while the Canadian Federation of Students and the New Democratic Party look longingly at European countries, where university is free, and demand that fees be lowered (forgetting that these systems have much less accessibility). Canadian provinces, except Quebec, have wavered between tuition freezes and moderate increases, while permitting much higher fees for career-focused programs such as MBAs and law. In the 1970s tuition fees covered about 20 per cent of the cost of running the universities. In 2008 they covered 50 per cent—a sharp rise that allegedly contains a substantial government subsidy for student participation.

Attending university can be quite expensive. The cost of tuition alone for a standard BA degree ranges from a low of $1,800 a year (two semesters) in Quebec to a high of $6,700 in Nova Scotia. But these numbers pale in comparison with the costs at elite American private schools, where tuition fees plus room and board in the region of $50,000 a year are standard. Specialized programs—medicine, law, or the MBAs offered at the top Canadian universities—can cost between $20,000 and $90,000 (for the Executive MBA), but relatively few students enter these programs.

Various kinds of financial support are available, ranging from entrance scholarships and bursaries to institutional and provincial government loans (the latter's student loan programs being heavily underwritten by the federal government). And more than half of all students work part time, on- or off-campus, while attending university. Summer jobs—and for those enrolled in special programs, co-operative education placements—allow students to learn and earn at the same time. And for anyone still short, banks and other financial institutions are ready with loans as well. There is also funding for special groups: First Nations students, for instance, are often funded by their bands, and there is also some funding available for the children of veterans, students with disabilities, and others. One difference between Canada and the United States, however, is that we do not offer nearly as much by way of athletic scholarships.

With all this support available, half of all students graduate from university without any debt. For the other half, the average debt now exceeds $28,000—a large but hardly crippling sum for someone with good lifetime career prospects. Universities worry about the amount of outside work students feel compelled to accept during the university year because jobs of more than ten hours per week can harm academic performance. But it's also clear that many students work for reasons of lifestyle as much as of necessity—to cover the cost of meals, drinks, cars, movies, and electronic gadgets.

The standard theory of supply and demand suggests that higher prices should drive down enrolment. In general, this does not appear to be the case. In fact, students fight to get into the really expensive programs like law and the MBA. If a university degree is half a private benefit and half a public good, and if students pay for about half the cost of their education, the fee structure would seem just about right. The real unfairness (see Chapter 17) is that the Canadian structure makes these fees cheaper for the rich than for the poor.

No One Agrees on What Students Should Know

Fifty years ago universities generally accepted that "every educated man" (shudder!) would know certain things. All students, regardless of program, studied a foreign language (French counted as "foreign"); arts students took a science course specially designed for them, and science students took English. At the graduate level there were similar requirements. A generation ago, PhD students had to demonstrate competence in not one, but two foreign languages (again counting French as foreign). The rationale for scientists was that a great deal of scientific research was published in, for instance, German. Historians needed to read the language of their particular field: Latin, or whatever.

What lay behind these requirements was the belief that there was a common body of knowledge that marked an educated person. Whether students agreed or not was irrelevant. That was the way things were, and at many places there were other compulsory courses: religion, physical education, philosophy, or psychology.

Most of this began to crumble in the late 1960s, when students' wishes began to be taken into account. They wanted to study what was "relevant" to them, not what some university committee thought they ought to know. The language requirement was dropped for undergraduates, and eventually at most places there were hardly any compulsory courses at all, except for English. Of course, if you are a sociology major, you have to take certain sociology courses, but otherwise you can choose what you please.

Debate about this issue has never died, and many universities have tried different ways to broaden students' experiences into disciplines they might not have chosen voluntarily. The University of Manitoba is currently doing interesting things in the area. At some places there is a "breadth requirement" that requires students to take at least one course from lists of physical and natural sciences, and from humanities and social sciences. Other universities have "core" or "foundation" courses that all students are required to take. There is talk of adopting the American liberal-arts model that has all students taking exactly the same courses in their first year (the University of King's College in Halifax does this), with Great Books and Great Ideas as a prominent feature.

This issue will never be resolved, because at its heart lies a simple question: Should students study what they want to study, or what universities think they ought to study? The question is easier to answer in the sciences, since there's consensus on what a physicist, a physician, or a mathematician needs to know—though less agreement on whether they should also take a course in English literature. In the arts and social sciences, however, there's very little agreement. If we had exclusive liberal-arts colleges that students were clamouring to get into, such places could impose a rigid curriculum on students, and some American colleges do this.

But in Canada, where the student as consumer of what universities have to offer is much more powerful, it's not likely that the old ways are going to return any time soon. Universities are smorgasbords for arts students: they can choose what they like, and they generally do. In this country—except for a certain level of literacy—there's currently nothing that all students should know.

6 Universities Don't Like Victory-Lap Students

This may seem hard to believe, but it's true: a quarter of students who qualify to graduate from high school don't graduate. Instead they come back to school and take some of their courses over again—not because they have to, but because they want to. This costs them nothing and is a ridiculous waste of public funds that distorts the university admissions process.

The standard scenario is simple. Mary and John both get 78 per cent in Grade 12 Math. Both want to be accountants. Mary's parents encourage her to graduate. She does so and applies to her top three universities. She is turned down by all of them and either goes to a lower-ranked school or shifts into a less-competitive program. John and his parents want into the top school. So he registers in Grade 12 again, takes a couple of courses, including Math 12, and gets his grade up to 85 per cent. He applies to university a year later, and, armed with two or three higher grades, he is accepted.

Both students have the same abilities in math. But John, having spent thousands of dollars of public funds, gets a higher grade on the second pass (easy to do, since it's the same material) and so gets into the premium university program. Since most universities accept the higher of the grades, he has played the system well, even though he has the same potential as Mary.

It's not just the public system that offers the victory lap. There are many private high schools, some entirely credible and offering top-quality education, others little more than grade-selling education mills. Students sign up for the extra courses in these private institutes, secure the higher grade through some combination of hard work, excellent tutelage, or teacher complicity, and apply to university with better scores.

This is a serious abuse, which universities could eliminate overnight by taking a few simple steps. First, they could announce that they will count only courses taken during the normal twelve years of study. Victory-lap courses would not be considered, except as evidence of students' determination to prepare themselves for advanced study. In the spring of 2012, the Ontario government announced as a cost-saving measure that students would not be permitted to take more than thirty-four credits in Grade 12 (they need thirty to graduate).

Public schools should also eliminate the practice of providing free courses for victory-lap students. If John is a late bloomer or changes direction late in his high school career, exceptions could be made. Otherwise, the courses should be offered on a cost-recovery basis.

The third solution, which we recommend in another chapter, would be the fairest: universities should establish their own entrance exams and simply ignore or seriously discount high school grades. These three actions—especially the third—would eliminate the academic incentives for redoing courses and remove the government subsidy for rule-bending grade-building. Admissions would be more equitable—Mary would have the same chance of getting into accountancy school as John—and one of the silliest aspects of admissions gaming will have been eliminated.

Your Grades Will Drop

Here's some really bad news for incoming first-year students: you are likely to do worse—sometimes much worse—at university than you did in your last year of high school. It's called "grade shock," and a July 2010 study in *Maclean's* published some alarming statistics on it. On average, half of students drop ten points from, say, 82 per cent to 72 per cent, or A– to B–. Nearly a quarter drop by two grade points, for example from A– to C–. Another quarter do about the same as in high school. Only a tiny minority, 2.5 per cent, see their grades improve.

Many students who have been awarded entrance scholarships lose them at the end of the first year because of lower grades. Alarmingly, those who come to university with the highest marks suffer the biggest drop. It comes, of course, as a tremendous shock to a student who is unprepared for it. The student is horrified and dismayed, and the parents who saw their son or daughter off to university with a scholarship in hand are disappointed. It's bad news all round. Students become discouraged, and many drop out at the end of their first year. In some programs nearly half the students who begin a first year don't come back for a second. What a waste of time, money, and human potential.

There's no secret about the cause of grade shock. Students aren't any stupider than they were fifty years ago, though more of the less able ones come to university than before. They do spend less time studying at university, but not enough to explain the phenomenon. It's not even that high schools are failing to prepare them, though this is probably part of it. The answer is grade inflation.

When you read that incoming students at UBC in 2010 had high school grades that averaged 87 per cent—up from 70 per cent in 1990, 80 per cent in 2000, and 85 per cent in 2008—you can see exactly what causes grade shock. There's also been some grade inflation at universities, but not as much. Inflated high school grades, fairly stable university grades. Thus the shock.

There was once a pretty good correlation between high school and university grades. Leaving aside students who came to university simply to

32

party, a top-notch high school graduate usually did well at university. In fact, quite a number did better at university, because in those days, high school students usually had to take subjects they weren't good at (typically math and science). When they got to university and didn't have to take them, their grades improved. This doesn't happen anymore, because they don't have to take high school math beyond a fairly basic level.

The figure of 92 per cent we mentioned in Chapter 1 for students entering McGill is bound to lead to grade shock and is absurd on the face of it. What will happen when the figure reaches 100 per cent? How will they assess incoming students? On their bowling scores? Our universities and high schools are complicit in a shameful fraud in which the worst victims are the students themselves.

What to Look for in a Prof

You are heading for your first year at university. You are excited, but a little anxious. What are your profs going to be like? Kind? Weird? Boring? Fascinating? Nasty? All of the above? Fortunately, if you have a choice, you can preview them by asking older students, and by checking ratemyprofessors.com, the website where students rate their teachers. Here's what to look for—the qualities that make a great prof.

Caring. Caring doesn't mean touchy-feely, but a genuine desire to see students succeed, and a willingness to make an effort to bring this about. It's more than friendliness, and it's a quality that not all profs have. Will the prof help you get work experience? Does she care about you as a person? Not all do. Student comments about the highest-rated profs always include this quality.

Engaging. Does the prof present the material in an interesting way? There's almost nothing worse than a boring instructor. You really know what Einstein meant by relativity when you experience an hour-long class that seems to go on for a day. Lecturing or running a lab or a seminar is a skill not all profs have. Does she have irritating habits? Does he say "um" five times in each sentence, or "in this instance" forty times in an hour (students keep score—these twitches can drive them crazy). Does he lecture with his back to the class?

Efficient. Is she well-organized? Does he take forever to grade papers and hand them back? If profs aren't efficient, it may be because they care more about their careers than about you. Beware.

Respectful. Does he think that teaching first-year students is beneath his dignity? Surprisingly, some profs do. Does she answer your questions without rolling her eyes? We hope so.

Fair. You may think you want a prof without strong opinions, political and otherwise, but you don't—such a person is the mental equivalent of a cabbage. You want one who won't downgrade you for disagreeing with him—neither some right-winger who marks your papers down for being too politically progressive, nor a Marxist who does the opposite. There aren't many of these, but to be stuck in a class headed by one is deadly.

Knowledgeable. This goes without saying, and almost all profs are.

Famous. You may think it would be great to be in a class run by Professor X, the internationally renowned scholar. Unfortunately, these people are rare, and they don't often teach first-year courses. Unless you are heading for graduate school and want to be able to say that you studied with the famous Professor X, this is a minor consideration.

We hope you find profs who have all these qualities. The good news is that universities take teaching much more seriously than they did a couple of generations ago. Most have "teaching and learning" centres that give courses on teaching techniques. Most let students rate profs anonymously at the end of the course, and sensible profs take the comments seriously. Things aren't perfect, but they are a great deal better than they used to be.

II
Planning a
University Career

The Million-Dollar Promise

Would you like to make a million dollars, maybe more? No problem. Paul Davidson, president of the Association of Universities and Colleges of Canada, has the secret: "While it is true that tuition has increased in recent years, so too has the value of a degree...University graduates will on average earn $1.3 million more during their careers than a high school graduate and $1 million more than a college grad."

Is the million-dollar promise something students can bank on, or is it misleading? University graduates, as a group, will indeed earn more than those without degrees. But if you ask if an individual student will make this much money, the answer is a resounding "maybe." The averages are accurate; but, as many university graduates have learned to their dismay, the university degree that leads to prosperity can also lead to unemployment, a string of part-time jobs or, more commonly in the midst of current economic times, underemployment—a low-paid, low-skilled position.

The kicker in all of this is the word "average." Yes, on average, someone with an undergraduate degree may well earn $1.3 more over a lifetime of work than someone with a high school diploma, and $1 million more than a college graduate. But the average is that of all university graduates, everyone from medical doctors, chemical engineers, accountants, lawyers compared to—which shall we pick?—graduates in dramatic arts or biology. Some lawyers, on the one hand, may well make $1.3 million in a couple of years (not forty). On the other hand, many people with other undergraduate degrees will struggle to find $30,000-a-year positions—leaving them just barely topping the average earnings of high school graduates. A heavy-duty mechanic can make as much as a university professor—just ask Bill's son-in-law. Averages are just averages.

While employment prospects for graduates in some fields are terrific—nanotechnologists, economists, and others have impressive career possibilities—the same is not necessarily true for graduates of many other academic programs. High-demand, high-quality programs, such as an MBA from an elite school or a medical degree, offer a high return on investment; others do not. An additional factor is student debt. About half of all graduating students carry student debt, and the average amount owed is $28,000. Imagine a worst-case scenario, in which a student takes more than four years to graduate, and accumulates a debt of $40,000, only to find herself underemployed as a barista, making $25,000 a year. What is the return on her investment in the first ten years after graduation? If she loved university, it may have been worth it, but if she had been seduced by the million-dollar promise, she has been badly deceived.

Think about these figures for a moment. Are music graduates, who average about $20,000 a year in their late twenties, going to make $1.3 million more over their careers than unionized construction workers? Obviously not, and of course no one gets a university degree in music for the money. For a musician, the million-dollar promise is irrelevant as well as false. Musicians do what they love to do.

Consider the situation facing newly minted teachers. Entry to a teachers' college is highly competitive, for teaching seems to hold out the prospect of a solid, well-paid, middle-class life. But demographic shifts have resulted in the closure of hundreds of schools and a great reduction in the number of teachers. According to the Ontario College of Teachers, 30 per cent of the 2010 graduating class in the province was unemployed the following year. Only 23 per cent of Ontario's new teachers had regular teaching jobs. The rest—almost half of the graduates—described themselves as underemployed, with only supply teaching or a job in a non-teaching field.

If universities were honest about the question of career opportunities and income, they would say this: "On average, our graduates do well economically. The top-performing students, particularly those in high-demand technical and professional fields, have very good employment prospects and will likely earn impressive incomes. Students in more general areas of study, and particularly those who fall short in motivation and work ethic, will likely struggle after graduation. Many of these students will, if academically capable, have to continue to an advanced degree; a growing number will have to continue their studies at a community college in order to prepare themselves for the work force. Plan accordingly." Doesn't have the same resonance and appeal as the million-dollar promise, does it?

For those ready for the challenge and the opportunity, university remains a special and wonderful option. If you are a young adult of broad curiosity, comfortable in the world of ideas and discovery, and want to explore the depth and breadth of the academy, then you are truly welcome on any campus, and you will leave richer for the university experience, whatever your later income may be. Start your academic career by doing careful research about the Canadian workforce, by adopting a skeptical approach to your choice of institution and program of study, and by reflecting very carefully on your reasons for attending university and your willingness to commit to the more-than-full-time job that is that of a motivated and devoted student. The intellectual benefits of a university degree are there for all the students who truly want them. Just don't count on that million dollars.

10 You May Need Two Degrees

For decades, a Bachelor's degree was a ticket to the middle class. Until the 1970s, only about 10 per cent of high school graduates went on to complete a Bachelor's, which meant that fewer than 5 per cent of the population had one. We also had a very middle-management kind of country—with lots of jobs in the growing public service, the banks, the large retail operations, and the big industrial concerns that drove the Canadian economy.

Three big things have happened since then. First, the national economy has changed, and middle-management jobs have eroded steadily. Second, specialization became the foundation of corporate and government operations. There was less interest in generalists and more urgency in hiring people who could move directly into a line position. Where previously a degree in any science or arts discipline was a fine career-launching pad, increasingly companies now look for marketers, human resources professionals, or financial analysts.

Third, and most important of all, Canadian universities flooded the market. The once-rare undergraduate degree became ubiquitous. With close to 50 per cent of all high school graduates going on to post-secondary education, what had once been a mark of distinction and accomplishment now became a base qualification.

Between 1998 and 2008 the number of degrees, diplomas, and certificates awarded at university level increased by 48 per cent. The undergraduate degree became what the high school diploma was in the 1960s, a general indication of intellectual ability and motivation, and the starting point for career development. Ironically, Canada has more need of people with trade skills than with basic undergraduate credentials, a fact brought into sharp relief by job listings in major employment markets.

Companies and government agencies that once happily hired from the newly minted undergraduate degree holders have raised their expectations. Why not hire someone with a Master's degree? Universities (and government funders) recognized what was happening and began a very rapid expansion of graduate programs. Between 1999 and 2009, full-time undergraduate enrolment increased by 43 per cent, but graduate enrolment shot up by 70 per cent.

Students seeking a good career now understand that two degrees are generally required if they want to increase their chances of success. Some go back to community college to get a practical credential, but most aspire to white-collar careers. With a few exceptions, such as engineering, the second degree or a Master's degree has become commonplace. The number pursuing discipline-based graduate degrees (English, botany, and such) has not grown all that much, but there is an enormous demand for what are called professional Master's degrees and professional degrees.

The silver lining here is that the impending retirement of the baby boomers should create a very large number of openings for young people. If the projections hold, students in the next decade will face abundant employment opportunities, and Canadian companies and agencies will be scrambling to find qualified, hard-working, dependable people. Indeed, the country is already short of skilled workers in many crucial, largely technical fields and encourages immigration to fill the slots.

It seems unlikely, however, that the graduation patterns from Canadian universities will match the changing employment needs. Canada produces too many generalists—the basic undergraduate degree holders—and not enough specialists, particularly in technical areas. Rick Miner, former president of Seneca College in Ontario, produced a crucial report in 2010 on the future of employment in Ontario. The title captured the situation very nicely: *People Without Jobs, Jobs Without People*. According to Miner, the Canadian education system is producing many well-educated people, but not necessarily in the fields where the need is the greatest. For Ontario alone, there may be as many as 800,000 vacancies by 2016 and two million by 2031—at the same time, unemployment rates will be growing dramatically.

Graduating students trying to make their way in an unfriendly and limited job market know and live the reality. The second degree has become a primary means of dealing with their career aspirations. It's clear, however, that universities and university students will have to continue to innovate and change if they are to keep up with the continually shifting economic situation.

Ask for Help If You Need It

Many university students struggle with their first year of study. There are various reasons for these difficulties, ranging from inadequate preparation, weak English skills, over-confidence, failure to attend classes and complete assignments, to being overwhelmed by the campus experience. Some groups—students from small and northern communities, Aboriginal students, international students, and math-deficient science students—are particularly at risk.

Traditionally, universities believed that students were responsible for their own academic progress and social adjustment. As young adults, they were left to fend for themselves, and those who were having difficulties were weeded out through mid-term collapses or first semester failures. However, because academic standards at secondary schools used to be higher than they are now, the dropout rates at most universities were fairly small. Consequently, universities saw no need to offer remedial assistance or to worry about student angst.

This is no longer the case. Universities are now expected to provide much more support by offering programs for at-risk students and help for students who get into trouble. Indeed, most universities now offer a variety of academic support programs designed to ease the transition into university or to assist students at academic risk. These range from "women in engineering" initiatives (offered because of the poor history of engineering in attracting and retaining female students) to rescue programs designed to help failing students re-establish their good academic standing, and even rooms full of cuddly puppies to interact with students stressed at exam time. International students are offered (at extra cost) English as a Second Language programs designed to bring them up to Canadian university language standards. All universities now have writing and math centres to assist students struggling with basic skills, although the writing centres rarely have enough money and staff to meet more than a tiny portion of the demand. (We pause to ask the usual English professor question: If there are so many university students in need of help with their writing, what were

42

our elementary and high schools doing with them for the previous twelve years?)

The impressive list of student support programs makes it clear that universities have accepted their responsibility to assist students in overcoming academic and personal difficulties. It is, of course, in their interest to do so. Universities spend a great deal of money and effort to recruit students; having them drop out after a single semester robs the institution of several years of tuition and grant revenue. Equally, universities are aware of the high personal and economic cost associated with failure—and they know that students who can be helped through the first year usually complete their programs.

The emergence of the culture of student support reflects, as well, the student-centred focus of the contemporary university. In the past, it was the students' responsibility to develop and maintain basic skills and to manage their own academic progress. In the past, there were no student assistance (or "Student Success") centres; those who needed help had to hire some needy graduate student to tutor them. All of that has changed: it is now a given that institutions share responsibility with students for their academic success.

However, with a few exceptions, universities are not proactive about drawing at-risk students into support programs. Aboriginal students are targeted early on in the process, to the point where some of them complain that they are stereotyped as weak and unlikely to succeed. International students often have ESL and orientation programs built into their first-year activities. More generally, however, student support programs require students to self-identify and opt in. This is a serious flaw in the process. Universities know students with low high-school averages (probably below 75 per cent for most programs) are at risk of failure; they should target these students for assistance before classes begin. Universities also know that students struggling in the first month of class often flounder their way to failure and that they have been conditioned, by the ever-forgiving world of Canada's K-12 system, to minimize their difficulties; here again, there should be programs of targeted support.

The problem, ultimately, is that some students have difficulty bridging the gap between the purveyors of tough love (the faculty) and the more compassionate and accommodating academic guides (the student-support programs). Students need to understand that they are on their own in terms of in-class performance, but that there is a great deal of help for those willing to ask for assistance. Unfortunately, many first-year students crash and burn academically before they discover that universities really are there to help.

First University, then College

This may be hard to believe, but it's true. Twenty years ago, the British Columbia Institute of Technology revealed that its largest single source for students was the graduating class of the University of British Columbia. Students with Bachelor's degrees were going back to school—and at a college, no less.

Such a thing was rare fifty years ago. Now, however, many university graduates go to college to transform their academic degree into a practical, employment-ready credential. Colleges are developing many one-year, post-degree programs specifically to meet this demand. They are much better than universities at connecting with employers—they are also more flexible in opening and closing programs, limiting and expanding enrolment, in line with realistic appraisals of job opportunities. For university students looking for work, college is a practical option.

Universities are uneasy about this trend. That fact that many university graduates "go back"—a weighted phrase—to college implies that universities have failed to prepare students for the job market. Governments resent paying twice for the same student: a full undergraduate degree and then a college diploma.

Colleges, though, like the arrangement. It provides them with a flow of well-educated, smart, and capable students who realize they need some practical training to get a job. Employers get employees who have both the technical proficiencies of a college degree and the broad skill set and understanding of the university student.

There has long been an unspoken hierarchy in post-secondary education. Colleges do the practical, remedial, and hands-on stuff. Universities do the cerebral, professional, leading-edge things. But this distinction misses the quality, difficulty, relevance, and attractiveness of many of the newer college programs. Few university degree programs in Canada match Sheridan College's animation program for student career prospects and employer satisfaction. In many of the technical fields, colleges offer excellent, demanding, and career-ready programs that remain in very high demand.

The sad part in this educational pattern is that it reveals a lack of planning and foresight. Some students, if they had thought carefully about their options, might have gone directly to college—a perfectly fine choice that does not get the respect it deserves. Other students who "go back" to college often look on their university years as a waste of time, but later discover that combining college and university education is an excellent way to proceed. If Canada's post-secondary institutions operated as a system, there would be greater co-ordination of the growing list of educational options. Since that will not happen, students will continue on winding, uncertain, and sometimes unnecessary educational journeys.

The Specialist Degree

If someone is planning to attend university in order to be assured of earning a good income, the specialist degree is the way to go.

In the highly diverse job market of the twenty-first century, many companies are seeking to fill niche positions, hoping to hire specialists who require minimal retraining to do their jobs. Firms that used to hire graduates for general management positions are increasingly looking for people with human resource management or marketing degrees for very specific jobs. In the high-tech sector, where start-up companies and leading-edge firms are working on the frontiers of science and technology, the need for specialists with degrees in systems design, nanotechnology, quantum computing, metallurgy, and the like is often acute. Students with specialist degrees that are directly connected to the marketplace can often find themselves in high demand.

However, specialist degrees are not the answer for everyone. Specialist degrees are primarily in technical areas; they typically require competence in Mathematics, Engineering, Applied Science, and Health Sciences, and thus may be an option for students with high school credits in math and science, strong technical aptitude, and scientific intelligence. Unfortunately for a great many students, few of these positions require a specific language ability or a Humanities or Social Science degree.

The challenge, particularly in these days of changeable job markets, is to figure out where the match is between interest, ability, and employment prospects. Since many students choose to attend university in the hopes of good future job prospects, it's surprising that students devote so little time to exploring job possibilities. The development of the international economy, particularly with the advent of more science and technology-based companies and jobs, is stretching the boundaries of the employment market and increasing the confusion between university degrees and employment prospects. The reality is that there are great jobs for graduates in the right fields, but bleaker prospects for those with degrees that, though personally and intellectually fulfilling, are not well connected to the marketplace. Universities usually leave it to students to determine their career path. Job-counselling services are available to students who seek them out; but, for some reason, most students don't make use of them and those who do tend to wait until their graduating year, when it is much too late to adjust program and course selection, co-ordinate job search and volunteer activities, and otherwise position themselves for a career in a specific field.

Students, especially those with the ability and desire to study in specialized fields, should, with their parents, start the process of finding the appropriate specialist degree or area of specialization early in their studies, ideally before they even start university. The number of jobs and careers in the marketplace is large and growing fast. Employment opportunities are as varied as the salary and working conditions. Career exploration requires an extensive winnowing exercise. Students, with advice from people who know the job market, should start by establishing initial parameters (science, applied science, humanities, fine arts, business, social science), specific job characteristics (inside job, outside job, large companies, entrepreneurship), specialized and personal skills sets (writing, public speaking, mathematics, technical innovation), salary expectations, work locations, and so forth.

This is a process, not a single decision. By the end of high school, students will probably not have made a final decision (parents are often more insistent on nailing a field down right away, often without taking aptitude and interest fully into account). The exceptions are those who from an early age have known exactly what they want to do: "I've always wanted to be a veterinarian"—those people presumably know what they need to study. Others should have identified specific areas of interest and skill—making sure that they push themselves to tackle areas that they can handle but that are challenging and lead where they want to go. Through ongoing self-evaluation, lessons learned in courses and programs, and continuing conversations with career specialists, students should narrow the options down. They should also use summer jobs, part-time work, volunteer activities, and extra-curricular opportunities to explore fields of potential interest.

For students who can follow it, this is good advice. Finding a good career, with solid job and income prospects, requires hard work and a certain amount of planning. Graduates are not entitled to a job and employers do not feel a responsibility to shift job descriptions to fit the employee's interest. A proper career search is not a one-time event or a single decision. To do it correctly, students should plan to devote a good deal of time and effort to exploring a complex and rapidly changing job market.

Universities Detest Helicopter Parents

She drove her daughter to the university and helped her move into residence. And then she wouldn't leave—her baby needed help adjusting to her first time away from home. So mummy stayed, sleeping on a mattress on the floor, for one week, then another, drawing complaints from students and irritating the residence managers. She left, reluctantly, after three weeks, at least partially confident her daughter was in good hands.

She was an extreme example of helicopter parents—people who hover over their university-age children—one of the strangest new aspects of university life. These are the same parents who produced the most cosseted children in history, coddled and pampered them from birth, and gave them all manner of material wealth and parental attention.

Now, two months after finally shepherding their children through high school, driving the teachers and administration half-crazy with their hovering, pestering, and general interference, they are being asked to stand down. The university wants to deal with the students—their legal clients—and not with parents. Shunted aside after years of providing a protective shell around their children, the parents don't know what to do. Universities are in a bind: they need parental money for tuition and residence fees. Other than that, though, the campus community wants the parents to keep their distance.

Helicopter parents, their hearts supposedly in the right place, like to interfere. Still thank heavens a small minority, they are quick to jump in if their kids fail a course, are accused of plagiarism, or otherwise run afoul of the university. They want to know their child is doing well. Some will call to check on class attendance and behaviour in residence. (We won't tell.) If Suzy fails a grade, the professor might well get a call and a demand for an explanation. In one well-remembered case, the mother admitted she had helped with research for a paper, assisted with writing, and proofread it carefully. She wanted a better grade for her work.

These parents can be tearful and soothing, or aggressive and demanding.

They are known to accompany children to on-campus job interviews and to insist on an explanation if the job is not offered. (Hint to parents: Showing up at the interview hurts the applicant. Stay away.)

These are the parents who walked their kids to school, would not let them go to the park until they were teenagers, and kept them under well-subsidized supervision until their late teens. The students, in turn, often lack an independence of spirit and turn readily to their parents for assistance long after the age when they should be independent.

Universities need to recognize the new parenting style and find ways to reach out to the helicopter moms and dads. Parents need to feel wanted, but they need to know that this hovering holds their children back and undermines the character-building aspects of the university experience. Universities could turn the situation to their advantage, as do American private schools, where these parents are seen not as pests but as potential major donors. Mommy and Daddy may find it hard to let go, but really, universities offer a great deal of support and encouragement.

Your baby has turned eighteen years old and is more than ready to leave the nest. Time to park the helicopter, turn off the engines, and sit back to enjoy the results of your nurturing.

 # It's About Careers, Not Education

A university education isn't what it used to be—and probably it never was! In an ideal world universities are about ideas, books, intellectual exchanges, and improving the world. In reality they are focused on training, career preparation, and various practical applications of theory—social work, education, or criminology. These are all good things, but they are often contradictory.

When universities talk about themselves, they speak of ideas, of the academy, of what they would call the "ivory tower" if that phrase had not gone out of fashion. They say that universities are for intellectual growth, for broadening minds, for "training people to think," for "life-long education," for equipping students with the intellectual skills to cope with a changing world. But what parents, governments, employers, and most students are looking for is preparation for a "meaningful" job, a well-paid one with regular hours where they get to tell people what to do and don't get their hands dirty. Applications for business programs flood in, and for career-focused degrees such as teaching, law, medicine, and information technology. Even the old disciplines of English and history have a large career-preparation aspect, for many students majoring in them plan to become schoolteachers.

In the 1970s, many young people came to university to learn about the world and to discuss "Big Ideas": the rights of women, homosexuals, and indigenous peoples; anti-colonialism; and early-stage environmentalism. Students hoped to change things for the better—and there were few enough of them that they could all find "meaningful" jobs.

The collapse of middle-class career opportunities in the 1980s and beyond altered the equation. People struggled to hold onto jobs through recessions and technological change. As the expansion of university education flooded the job market, suddenly a university education was no longer a virtual guarantee of career options.

Now it seemed that everyone had a degree, and there was talk that the MA was the new BA (see Chapter 10). One result was that even more young people came to university, since a degree was now the first filtering device for job applicants, as a high school diploma had been in the 1940s. As well, students became far more career oriented in their choice of program: if environmentalism was big, bring on a degree in environmental engineering; if the lumber industry was in the doldrums, forget the BSc in Forestry. Business schools flourished as never before.

But the universities remained largely locked in the 1960s and were unable to change quickly. While students began to flock to career-oriented disciplines, there was an oversupply of philosophy professors and too few in business.

The sad thing here is that a good liberal arts and science graduate is a great employee. Find a graduate who loves to learn, who reads well, thinks critically, and communicates effectively (not all of them, certainly), and you have a young adult who can go places. A philosophy or physics grad, properly equipped and motivated, is as valuable to employers and to society as any graduate of a practical or technical program. Brains are brains, and reasoning is reasoning—the skills are transferable. If we can figure out how to flag these great graduates, they can have it all: a terrific education and a start on a great career.

Educated and Underemployed

Each year more than 250,000 Canadians graduate from university, parts of a new class of young citizens whose education is poorly matched with the national economy. Half of them carry debt, averaging $28,000. These people have a variety of options. They can continue their studies at the graduate level, hoping that an additional credential will generate better opportunities. They can go to a trade or career-oriented program at one of the country's excellent colleges. According to the National Graduates Survey of the Class of 2005, 13 per cent of university graduates continued their studies at a college. The other option is to head into the workforce. Those who do this have encountered surprising difficulties, struggling to find paid employment or, in close to a third of the cases, accepting unskilled, low-paid work to pay the bills. Imagine working for $10 or $12 an hour to support yourself, with $28,000 or more of debt to pay off.

The majority of Canadians believe in the value of a university education—if not to strengthen the Canadian economy, then simply for personal gain. Surveys of Canadian high school students and their parents consistently show that most believe that high school graduates should have a university education. A Nova Scotia study, "Youth Decision Survey" (2010), showed that 60 per cent of high school students believed their parents wanted them to go to university. Statistics Canada reported in 2010 that 67 per cent of parents wanted their children to go to university, while 15 per cent hoped for a college or CGEP diploma.

But here is the shocker. A mere 2 per cent wanted their kids to get a trades qualification. Skills/Compétences Canada reports that some 40 per cent of new jobs created in Canada in the next decade will require a trade. Even now, thousands of skilled trades' and highly specialized technical jobs go unfilled in this country: the Merit Contractors Association of Saskatchewan reported in July 2012 that 75 per cent of its members were having trouble hiring journeypersons when they needed them, and 40 per cent couldn't find them at all. Some firms have started recruiting in Romania. In the classified ads in major city newspapers, there are many jobs in advanced manufacturing, computer-based work, construction, and healthcare. But for those with a basic Bachelor's degree in English, Chemistry, Outdoor Recreation, or Psychology, jobs that fit a graduate's qualifications are very hard to find.

Students completing degrees in applied and specialized disciplines generally do fine; petroleum engineers are pulling in lots of job offers and high starting salaries, and accounting graduates often have jobs lined up before they graduate.

It is those with non-specialized degrees—the "garden-variety" graduates with Bachelor's degrees in the Arts and Sciences—who face the very real prospects of prolonged unemployment or underemployment. According to James Côté, author of *The Hidden Crisis in the Canadian University System* and co-author of *Ivory Tower Blues*, our universities produced some 1.2 million graduates in the 1990s. In the same decade, about 600,000 jobs were created that actually required undergraduate credentials. While these university graduates are less likely than high school graduates to be unemployed, this is because they often accept jobs actually requiring lower levels of education. They are, in effect, underemployed, trading their university degrees for the chance to compete for unskilled work.

Côté calls this the "downward cascading effect" of credential overproduction. The current unemployment rate among university graduates is only 4.4 per cent, though it's undoubtedly higher for recent graduates (unemployment for all Canadians age fifteen to twenty-four is now 14 per cent). What is more significant is the estimated underemployment rate: 35 per cent, according to the OECD. In this, Canada ranked second only to Spain in a 2010 survey by *The Economist*.

The mix of unemployment and underemployment—together totalling perhaps half of all university graduates looking for work—calls into question the national belief that personal choice trumps all other considerations at university. Students are encouraged to study what they want—self-actualization is as strong in universities as it is in high schools—rather than focus their studies on what the economy needs. This means the shape and skillset of the Canadian workforce is largely set by the decisions of tens of thousands of eighteen-year-old, first-year students. If they choose the Humanities or basic Science, when there is a need for engineers and nurses, the economy suffers, and so do they.

Many countries, from India to the Baltic states, deal with this by directing students into high-need areas. In Estonia, to use a little-known example, the government subsidizes all of the seats in high demand areas; those wishing to study other fields pay the full cost. Students are not prevented from following their intellectual noses, but they may end up doing so at their own expense.

Students and parents have responded to the situation by demanding low tuition fees—particularly in Quebec—and more access to university, two conditions that will produce even more graduates and further erode the quality of undergraduate education. By fighting for those outcomes they are missing the point of the problem. As many of the Quebec students will discover upon graduation, anger about a small increase in tuition will not solve their real problems, which rest with adaptation to the workforce.

Students and parents need to align their aspirations with employment realities; though, admittedly it can be difficult to know what these realities are, when even governments aren't sure, and universities, whose main goal is to fill their programs, won't or can't tell. Clearly though, there are some major indicators: you'd have to be foolishly optimistic to expect to coast into a teaching job in southern Ontario any time in the near future. Governments need to ensure that the post-secondary system produces the workers the country needs. Universities hold tightly to what is dear to them: the idea of the university as a place of learning, self-discovery, and global awareness—not career preparation. They are uncomfortable with the reality that, in most fields, they are chiefly job training institutions. Until they and the public accept this fact and act on it, the disconnection between the world of work and the academy will continue to grow, and so will public dissatisfaction.

University Fees are Discriminatory

What percentage of the costs of running a university do you think have anything to do with the undergraduate experience? There's quite a list of things that don't: graduate teaching, faculty sabbaticals, faculty research time (the argument goes that faculty research improves the undergraduate experience, but this is unproven), research laboratories and offices, library holdings that mainly benefit graduate students and faculty members, expensive scientific equipment and the support staff needed to run them, as well as university research, fundraising, alumni, recruiting, and commercialization offices.

None of these has much to do with undergraduates, yet undergraduates pay 50 per cent of the costs of operating the entire university—they may pay 80 per cent or more of the cost of the teaching and other services that are targeted directly at them. And low-income students are more likely to be undergraduate than graduate students.

No less a left-wing icon than Bob Rae has accurately described low tuition fees as one of the largest tax transfers to the upper-middle class in the country. It's not just a matter of saving students, or the taxpayers, money. There are broad socio-political issues connected with the question. Canadian university students come disproportionately from the ranks of the upper- and upper-middle classes. Children of the poor and lower-middle class are significantly less likely to attend university. Even with the availability of student loans, bursaries, university scholarships, and the like, poor families are much less likely to send their children to university.

It follows that the incentives for post-secondary education go dispro-portionately to the rich. They can shelter money in Registered Educational Savings Plans, which provide tax-free interest savings when applied to education. The Government of Canada supplements those contributions with a payment of 20 per cent (up to $400 a year) to encourage more sav-ing. Guess which economic group is more likely to put money aside for its children's university education, the single parent earning $30,000 a year or the two-income family pulling in $150,000?

Because fees are deductible, a wealthy family will pay some $2,600 a year less for its child to attend university than will a poorer family. This is why Bob Rae expressed such dismay at the NDP's continued insistence on lower university tuition fees, which remain a major subsidy for the wealthiest people in the country.

Canada's supposedly fair approach denies universities the tuition money that they need—and that many students can afford to pay—while not ensuring that students from poorer families can actually afford to attend university. We offer the promise of inclusiveness, but provide inequal-ity of opportunity. Canada's best option would be to allow tuition fees to increase dramatically but to require universities and/or government bursary and loan schemes and grants to help students from lower-income backgrounds. A $10,000 tuition fee is as affordable for wealthy families as a $2,000 a year charge is for poor families.

Instead of tinkering with existing student loan arrangements—which can be very complex and often don't help those in greatest need—a program of financial assistance for students from low-income families is required. Without a real change like this, coupled with a major outreach initiative to reach the parents and school counsellors of these young people, the Canadian university system will become even more guilty of abetting income inequality in Canada.

Changing the system so that students from poor families actually have a greater chance of attending university would also address one of the greatest inconsistencies and shortcomings of the Canadian university sys-tem—namely, that they have increasingly become subsidized job-training institutions for our wealthier fellow citizens. But this is unlikely to happen: the middle classes won't like it at all, and they are the ones who vote.

III
Inside the Ivory Tower

18 Not Every University Is "World Class"

"Excellence" is a word universities use a lot. The students are excellent, the faculty is excellent, and the facilities are excellent (except when they need more money, in which case they are substandard). Overall, they are "world-class," which is even better than excellent. But are they all equally excellent? Of course not, but you would never know it from promotional materials and presidential speeches.

Maclean's annual ratings—hated by all universities except the ones that top the list—tell us that this is not so. Employers know it's not so, as do the students who are aware enough to care. And faculty members know there's a pecking order.

Canada prizes and demands equality of access and treatment—in universities as much as in health care. But all Canadians know that for first-rate care their children are better off at Sick Kids in Toronto than at the hospital in The Pas, Manitoba. So it is with universities.

The gap between the top Canadian institutions and the rest is growing. Not so long ago, working conditions, wages, and research opportunities (but not libraries and laboratories) were fairly equal across the country. No longer. Programs such as the Canada Research Chairs have shovelled huge resources into the high-ranked places—the so-called "medical-doctoral institutions." These places also benefit the most from fundraising campaigns. The myth that all Canadian universities are equally excellent persists, but the reality is very different.

Canadian universities have not admitted publicly that there is a large diversity of experience and performance in our institutions. A 2010 report on universities declared, "all Ontario universities are research intensive." This is nonsense. The University of Toronto is research intensive. Algoma University is not.

American schools figured this out long ago. In the United States, there's a wide diversity among colleges and universities. Junior colleges focus on teaching lower-income kids at academic risk, and they don't expect their faculty to do much, if any, research. Expensive liberal arts colleges emphasize high-quality instruction and a rich student experience. Medical-doctoral institutions are research powerhouses.

The United States has many rating systems. If your alma mater is not a top-ranked research school or academically strong, it might be a top party place or have the best sports teams. No one thinks that the (fictional) University of Southern North Dakota is the same as Yale. But Americans do understand—much better than Canadians—that any one of a hundred small colleges may be a better place for some students than the Ivy League and research-intensive schools.

But not in egalitarian Canada. Here, everyone is excellent at, it seems, everything. Save for *Maclean's* and an effort by the *Globe and Mail* to rank the student experience, we seem to disavow hierarchies of achievement and quality, even if we know in our hearts they are there.

The plain fact is that not all places are excellent, nor (by definition) can they all be above average. The academic ability of the students at Waterloo is better than those at the University of Winnipeg. Researchers at Dalhousie outperform their provincial counterparts at Cape Breton University. The quality of the student experience at Acadia is much superior to that of York, and Mount Allison develops much stronger loyalty than mega-versities like the University of Alberta. That's just the way it is, and it's not necessarily a bad thing.

Great things are happening at all institutions. Weaker students can get strong assistance at open-access institutions like Brandon and the

University of New Brunswick, Saint John. Regina is no McGill, but in select areas (police studies, Great Plains research) it is the best in Canada. The sense of community is much better at the University of Saskatchewan than at the University of British Columbia. The law school at the University of Victoria isn't as well known as the University of Toronto's, but in fields like Aboriginal law it is outstanding. Aboriginal students are well supported at the University of Northern British Columbia; Vancouver Island University and Thompson Rivers University serve international students superbly.

Canada needs to drop the preoccupation with similarity and abandon the language of uniform excellence. Universities must focus on the specific qualities and abilities of their students, the problems and opportunities of their host region, and the limits of their resources. They need to celebrate their specific identities and strengths, not parrot fairy tales about the uniform excellence and similarity of the Canadian post-secondary system.

Our Universities Need a Proper Admissions Test

Canadian universities educate and train undergraduates. Their raw material is high school students. Universities know how to select the students by themselves and could easily do so if they wanted to. But they don't, and won't.

Instead universities let high schools and high school teachers perform this critical function. But why? Why do they outsource the single most important decision in their operations? Universities in general have strong reservations about the value of high school grades, even though they won't say so in public. Despite this, high school grades are the main criterion used by universities to evaluate applications.

There are other ways of doing things. Many American universities combine results from Standardized Aptitude Tests (SAT) with high school grades (or GPAs, grade point averages, as the universities call them). Some require essays as well. Others ask for lengthy personality profiles and face-to-face interviews. The top Japanese schools have their own entrance exams, for which applicants have to pay up to $1,000 for the privilege of writing. At places like Yale or Duke it often helps to have a parent who went there too, and then gave the place millions! That makes you a "legacy student," and you go to the head of the line. We don't recommend this—buying your way into university seems just too un-Canadian.

Our schools, in contrast, rely on a single set of numbers, produced by people over whom the universities have no control. By adopting this method of doing things Canadian universities have chosen to play a minimal role in the selection of their own students. It's amazing that universities have so little control over the calibre of incoming students. Imagine any other business turning over its quality control to a separate agency with a demonstrably uneven track record.

The solution is simple. Universities can establish their own admission tests. They can do this individually or collectively. The tests can be faculty- or program-specific, generic, scholarly, personality-based, or some combination of these. Students can be charged for writing the exam (to cover marking and administration costs). A private SAT-type service could be provided, or the universities could do all the testing themselves, according to their own requirements and standards. Open-entry institutions wouldn't need such an admission test, although its absence would draw attention to their lower standards.

Universities need basic information about applicants. Can they read at an advanced level? Can they write effectively? Do they have the necessary reasoning, numeracy, and analytical skills? Are they keen on learning what the university has to teach? Specialized programs, such as engineering and architecture, will have special questions to ask. The results of these tests, reviewed and analyzed over time, will provide valuable input into the admissions process.

This is not a new concept, even for Canada. Most law schools in the country require students to write the Law School Admission Test (LSAT). Architecture schools and some accounting programs have entrance tests.

Medical schools, of course, put applicants through a rigorous and intense exam and interview process.

A handful of elite universities—three or four to start—should break out from the pack. They claim they want the best scholars. They should prove it. If the top institutions implemented a test, the best students would still apply. A high school graduate is not going to switch from Toronto to Laurentian just because there is a three-hour test to write to get into the U of T.

Universities need to reclaim full responsibility for their admission decisions. They should pick students with a high chance of succeeding. Admission tests will do this. At the very least, they will give universities less reason to whine about the dismal standards of high schools.

Why will there be no admission test any time soon in Canada, outside the professional programs? One reason is that, unlike the situation in the United States, even the best Canadian universities don't have huge numbers of applicants. Unlike the elite American places, they don't turn down 90 per cent of their applicants, and they don't want to discourage any student from applying.

It's significant too that these admission tests come from the United States—and "American-style" is one of the worst things you can say about an idea in much of Canada. Why not let everyone have a chance at the University of Toronto? That's the Canadian way. Too bad. Universities will continue to outsource admission decisions, much to the detriment of many students and the universities themselves.

Our Math Students Just Can't Compete

A few years back, the *Japan Times* ran a story about the status of math education in that country that included a copy of a math exam. Math teachers in the United States remarked that the test looked like a first-year university final math exam. In fact, the test was from the compulsory national examination—not a tough one given to science students, but a much easier one given to high school students planning to study humanities at university. Humanities!

We live in a scientific age, where a high level of mathematical literacy is essential for national competitiveness in the fast-moving new economy. Stock markets work at hyper speed, driven by complex algorithms. The digital media sector requires thousands of workers with mathematical abilities. Engineers and applied scientists are needed in huge numbers to capitalize on the commercial possibilities of clean technology, biotechnology, nanotechnology, and many other science-based -ologies. Numeracy and mathematical ability are essential in business—particularly in accounting. They play a critical role in medicine and health care, and are increasingly important in the social sciences. Math has emerged as a core requirement for jobs in our modern economy.

Canadian thirteen-year-olds are ranked eighteenth in the world in both math and science by the *Trends in International Math and Science Study*. In a different study, we ranked tenth in math skills in 2009, down from seventh three years earlier. Results are not even across the country. Alberta tops the Canadian rankings, and urban schools do better than rural ones.

But the major issue for Canada is that not enough students are going into math-based undergraduate and graduate degrees. An astonishingly high percentage of Math PhD candidates at North American universities are international students. Would you have guessed more than 90 per cent? There is an ethnic twist to this issue as well. Students of Asian ancestry, particularly new Canadians, dominate the enrolment in Canadian universities in math.

Canadian faculties of math, computer science, and engineering work very hard to attract more Canadian students. The University of Waterloo's Faculty of Mathematics—the largest in the world—operates an international test of mathematical proficiency and received a multi-million dollar grant from the Gates Foundation to expand the global reach of the examination. Other schools try just as hard and make substantial—and only marginally successful—efforts to attract more female students. But the main point is that there are not enough Canadian math students at Canadian universities.

Explanations abound: poor teaching in elementary and high school, poor instruction at university, a subject matter that many students find unappealling, an absence of role models for young math scholars, a male/geek culture that repels women, and a weak understanding of career opportunities in the field. The lack of student interest is not new, which means parents are not always helpful or academically supportive. Perhaps there is a simpler explanation: math is hard and requires a lot of work. Class work must be supplemented by hours of practice and repetition.

Canada needs to make major advances in math education and to engage students in math. The country needs a significant improvement in the emphasis given to mathematics and related fields in high schools. Improving the training and professional development of math teachers would help. Universities should require Grade 12 math for applicants to all programs and program-specific math courses should be required across the university.

More importantly, the country needs a fresh approach to math education. Numeracy is as important as literacy in the twenty-first century. National competitiveness requires Canadian students to be prepared for the realities of the modern workforce. Without a substantial increase in the number of math-savvy graduates, Canada will have difficulty attracting and holding new-economy and tech-based companies in the country.

Killing the Traditional Disciplines

What do we mean by traditional disciplines? We mean those disciplines that date from the nineteenth century, when universities escaped the control of the churches and began to teach literature, history, and the social, natural, and physical sciences. These are, or were, the core disciplines at Canadian universities.

Up to 1960 this core was unchallenged, with the addition of new social sciences (sociology and psychology, for example), new professional disciplines (nursing, education, architecture), and new physical sciences deriving from new discoveries (nuclear physics). The vast majority of students studied in the central academic fields. Emerging interdisciplinary programs in the 1960s and 1970s—Canadian studies, Native studies, women's studies, labour studies, and the like—had a relatively small impact.

In the past twenty years, students have been voting with their feet for disciplines that promise lucrative careers. New fields like business and commerce have grown rapidly—more business degrees are granted each year in North America than Bachelor of Arts degrees. The traditional disciplines reacted by creating new interdisciplinary programs, like international studies, law (as an undergraduate degree, a huge success at Carleton University), criminology or legal studies, administrative studies (one of the largest majors at the University of Western Ontario), and degrees oriented towards the helping professions and preprofessional programs.

Canada has so far avoided excesses such as the Bachelor of Surf Science at Edith Cowan University in Australia, but new program development has continued apace. The percentage of students majoring in traditional disciplines—particularly in the languages and literature programs—continues to drop, in some cases sharply. As a result, academics in these fields seek new ways of packaging and presenting their material in the hope of attracting student attention. Some of these new initiatives draw on contributions from the traditional disciplines and are demanding, intellectually exciting, and very career focused, including programs in nanotechnology, digital media, gerontology, and various branches of environmental studies. Critics see others as academically weak, lacking in rigour, and overly focused on faddish student interests—studying comic books or the Harry Potter novels in English departments, for example.

External support matters, too. Business schools have been bolstered by substantial amounts of government funding, employer demand, and donor support. Only one arts faculty—the Irving K. Barber School of Arts and Sciences at UBC Okanagan—has attracted similar support.

The shift in student and public interest, and the loss of centrality for the traditional disciplines, presents universities with a huge challenge. The old disciplines have been around for a long time by Canadian standards, and the fences that separate and protect them are high. Most administrative and faculty resources are based in the standard disciplines, even if the students are flocking to new fields. Professors from the older disciplines still dominate the decision-making committees, making it tough to reallocate resources to growing programs.

With students (and often government funding and employer interest) focused in one direction, and with university resources and priorities focused in different ones, universities are caught in a dilemma. Change is difficult and in a way undesirable, for traditional scholarly values and approaches are a strength of the university system. Universities are being torn in two directions, with powerful forces of tradition (disciplines, academic departments, and established programs) aligned in opposition to equally powerful forces for change (employers, students, and interdisciplinary scholars seeking to break away from the standard fields). There's no easy solution to this problem.

The Sad Decline of University Outreach

One of the greatest innovations in higher education was the American land-grant university system, founded by acts of Congress during the Civil War. These publicly funded universities were given large land endowments in return for a commitment to work to with their region to promote economic and social development. The result was an inspiring demonstration of the effectiveness of academic research and university outreach.

Canada's early public universities followed a similar approach. Faculties of Agriculture and Engineering worked closely with farmers, business, and industry. Scholars in health and home economics aided society in many ways, most notably by improving maternal health and general well-being.

Campus outreach or extension operations enjoyed widespread support at the university and generated a great deal of interest in the communities. The universities demonstrated their relevance on a regular basis, often with spectacular results, (i.e., the impact of western universities on prairie agriculture).

Outreach operations have had a tough run in recent years. Programs have been cut back, staff allocations reduced, and budgets slashed. There are notable exceptions, such as St. Francis Xavier University's Antigonish Centre and Memorial University's strong commitment to participation in the health of small communities. For the most part, though, universities don't do much of this sort of thing and, beyond a few community activists, most faculty members have little interest in community engagement.

Canada's research-granting agencies (SSHRC, CIHR, and NSERC) are sending strong signals to university faculty. Preference is being given to work that emphasizes community outreach and to programs that require extensive community partnerships. As clear as they have been, these messages have not been well-received.

Outreach has become a low priority for individual faculty members and for institutions. The standard measures of success—academic papers and grants—bear little connection to time-consuming outreach activities. For career advancement and institutional prestige promotion, faculty efforts are focused on purely scholarly pursuits. To put this in concrete terms: a junior assistant professor of chemistry may be strongly interested in participating in the local high school science fair, but when promotion time comes around she will be judged, not on her community service (despite that 20 per cent of her job description involves such activity), but on her publication record. Publishing in scientific journals will boost her career, and if she publishes less, to spend more time with the science fair, her career will suffer.

With universities cutting back on outreach activities, private consultants and networks of non-governmental organizations have emerged to fill the gap. These NGOs, often highly motivated, low-cost, and professionally engaged, have emerged over the past forty years to work with communities, local organizations, and cultural groups. The flooding of the community assistance market by consultants and NGOs has left a smaller niche for universities; unfortunately, even that niche is being left unfilled.

In the long run, the retreat from outreach will not serve universities well. For decades, the operations of extension divisions and off-campus faculty engagement helped buttress public support for Canadian universities. Academic research was relevant, readily available, and of real impact. If university scholarship has seemed to become irrelevant, marginal, and "only academic," universities should be concerned.

Academic outreach is not entirely dead; some individuals and programs still make determined efforts to connect with community. These people often have real impact and gain enormously from the experience, through personal as opposed to institutional rewards. In time, universities may rediscover the values of community outreach and realize that sharing and participating in community issues is central to their mission and value to society. For now, the increasingly inward-looking universities are, unwisely, cutting themselves off from their regions and undermining the support of those who in the final analysis, pay to keep them open.

23. A Nasty Secret

There's a nasty secret that rarely surfaces in public discussions about universities. Many students—at some places perhaps nearly half of all of those who enter—do not graduate. Across the country, tens of thousands of students each year leave campuses, some to transfer to other educational institutions, others for jobs. But the vast majority leave as academic failures.

Think about that for a moment. Remember how much time and effort young Johnny devoted to picking a university, paying tuition and room and board, and launching his studies? Now, imagine how he feels when he fails three or four mid-term exams, struggles with essays and lab reports, crashes during final tests, and then gets the dreaded Dean's letter requiring an extended academic holiday, often in mid-year when his probation runs out. Contemplate the phone call: "Hi, Mom. I got kicked out of school. Can I come home?"

So much is loaded into this experience. Forget the money; you can write that off as an unfortunate investment. Remember that young people, coddled from birth, have little experience with failure. They have been told that prosperity and opportunity require a university degree. They know their future depends on it. And now they have been rejected by the institution that was the repository of their career ambitions. Failure in university is a life-limiting experience.

Why is the failure rate so high? Even the best schools, attracting only the top students, lose up to 10 per cent of their first-year students. Issues of maturity, too much beer, the discovery of sex, wrong program choices, laziness, homesickness, and money woes are part of the challenge.

But the real culprit is the national conceit that all students who want to go to university should have the chance. University, according to this belief, is a right, like shelter and medical care. Other countries limit access to (publicly funded) universities to students who have demonstrated aptitude and motivation.

No such elitism for Canada. Even the top schools are comparatively accessible. Our national mantra about equality of opportunity is no better displayed than through the expensive university admission processes. Universities need money to survive. Students provide money. Therefore students are heartily welcomed, with inadequate concern about their ability to succeed.

The current approach is wrong. Students who fail carry a heavy personal burden. Their parents are disappointed—with their child or the institution—as well as out of pocket. The cost to government is considerable. And classes with large numbers of students ill-suited for study can produce a very unhappy academic environment.

There is enormous variation in academic success rates. Universities that attract more students of lower academic achievement (below 75 per cent is a good cut-off, given today's grossly inflated high school grades) have lower graduation rates. The data on this crucial topic is collected but is rarely disseminated and does not form part of the *Maclean's* ranking of universities—even though it may be the single most important measure of institutional effectiveness.

Greater honesty is needed here. A dismally large portion of the students going to a Canadian university in any academic year will not graduate. If incoming students knew this secret, some of the weaker ones might find a better training option elsewhere. Others might be more motivated and might work harder, knowing how many actually do fail and are asked to leave. This dirty little secret needs to be aired.

Gypsy Administrators

Canadian universities used to be run by people who, like the generals in a democratic army, had begun as private soldiers and then had been promoted up through the ranks: from faculty member to department head (not chair), associate dean, dean, vice-president, and president. Sometimes outsiders were brought in, but these were exceptions.

The system was stable but it was far from perfect. Department heads often were appointed without term and could spend years, or even decades, in the position, sometimes until well past their "best before" dates. Before tenure became common after World War II, department heads had tremendous power over the careers of faculty members (as did the deans, who also often served for long periods). But they did know their institutions very well, and were devoted to the universities` well-being. Usually they did not serve with one eye on the next promotion or, in the case of presidents, a call from a more prestigious institution. They were also well-known and respected citizens of their communities.

The change started at the highest level, the presidencies, and at the largest and most prestigious institutions. As part of the change, universities began relying upon the services of search consultants, the largest and best known of which is Janet Wright and Associates. This company has been credited with making the university search process commonplace. Companies like this are not cheap; they typically charge over $100,000 to find the perfect president for the university.

Two other developments changed the dynamics of the field: a sharp rise in administrative salaries and other benefits for senior university officers (some American university presidents make over $1 million a year, and their Canadian equivalents are reaching the $500,000 mark); and rising demands and expectations on academic administrators. By the early twenty-first century, a large group of academic administrators had emerged. Their skills rested in academic planning, faculty management, government relations, fund-raising, and community outreach. Sometimes they had served in the ranks, but quite often they were the products of Human Relations or business enterprises. They moved with increasing regularity from campus to campus, increasing the cross-fertilization of ideas, procedures and processes, and professionalizing senior administration in the process. What they did not have, though, was a long association with and a strong loyalty to any particular institution. Like large corporations, universities were coming to believe in the value of new blood and the transferability of administrative talent.

Canada now has an impressive group of "gypsy administrators," although not as large and mobile as in the United States. (Full disclosure: Ken has been one of these, in Canada and in New Zealand.) They move from campus to campus, moving up either the administrative ladder to higher positions or from small, less-prestigious institutions to higher-profile campuses. The emergence of an administrator network, bound by national associations of deans, vice-presidents, and presidents, has professionalized university administration and ushered in an era of systematic management that reflects the growing complexity, importance, and competitiveness of the field.

The advent of these administrators is not without its costs. Sometimes the search process goes badly wrong. When a new university president leaves after a year or two—one year for the university to discover a mistake has been made and they've wasted their $100,000 and a second year to buy out the president's contract and send him on his way—the resulting controversy (often generated because of the size of the payout) highlights the negative side of this recent trend. New officials can bring new and fresh—or recycled—ideas with them, but they can also struggle to get to know the local environment. As the focus shifts to academic and governmental metrics and away from serving the area, longstanding hallmarks of the Canadian university system (local knowledge, ties to their community, and commitment to the region) are either compromised or lost altogether.

In contrast to most management posts, where one reports to a supervisor or boss, university administrators report both up (to university senates) and down (to the faculty with whom they work). Certainly, the administrators' ability to keep their jobs is dependent upon ongoing support from the faculty. Complex review procedures—at the University of Victoria, managers seeking reappointment have to be confirmed by 60 per cent of those voting—put severe constraints on administrative independence. Administrators are often advised by their bosses or supporters to slow down controversial changes, even if urgently needed, to secure reappointment.

These senior jobs, although attracting a sizeable number of applicants, are increasingly hard to fill with top people. Senior administrators are well paid, but the work is extremely demanding (some describe the primary job of a university president as "herding cats"). Working hours are long, meetings are seemingly endless, resources are limited, and expectations are very high. Inevitably, they must also deal with the few faculty members who are serious troublemakers, take up a lot of time, and are virtually impossible to get rid of.

So long as universities remain focused on enrolment targets, research grants and publication rates, the reliance on gypsy administrators will likely continue. Those institutions that emphasize regional commitment and community engagement will, and probably should, place greater importance on building from within and on valuing local contacts. Given the current university environment, however, it is likely that the pool of willing and able candidates will remain small and that universities will compete amongst themselves for the small number of truly talented academic administrators in the country.

We Aren't Producing Engaged Citizens

Universities were going to change the world. It was the 1960s and social ferment was everywhere. Women were under-represented. Bring them in—and in they came. Minorities had too small a place on campus. Open the doors—and in they came. Subtle and not so subtle restrictions limited opportunities for Jews, Aboriginal people, and others. Change the rules, be accessible—and changes were made. Ensure people of working-class backgrounds could afford to go to university, and that they knew of the opportunities. Money was found—and openings created. Satellite campuses were built in smaller communities to increase accessibility. Done and done again.

The promoters of the university system got all they asked for and more, but did education transform the nation and the world? Participation rates soared, accessibility expanded, new groups of students attended, and radical academic perspectives replaced stodgy orthodoxy. On the social front, universities have been at the forefront of many key revolutions—gay rights, women's rights, Aboriginal rights—and have established traditions of acceptance and tolerance that, though hard won, have been replicated outside the campuses. Racism has moderated, or at least gone underground. More students have access to the economic opportunities attainable through advanced education, although these seem to be backsliding of late. Graduates seem to have been well trained for jobs. There is much on the positive side of the ledger.

But the good news seems to have faded. Participation rates in politics, particularly through elections, are woefully bad and getting worse. Civic responsibility, as seen through charitable donations and volunteerism, is far from impressive (a quarter of the population does most of the giving). Interest in international affairs remains amazingly marginal—particularly surprising given the multicultural nature of the population. The country's devotion to innovation—and, indeed, the country's commitment to the concept of Canada—seems fragmented at best. When was the last time

Canadians got truly excited about a new national initiative? Ask Stéphane Dion what the country thought of the "Green Shift."

Contrast the 2010s with the 1970s. Forty years ago, universities in Quebec led the political turmoil of Quebec separatism. Western Canadian universities were at the forefront of the western alienation debate (the University of Calgary has maintained a reputation in this regard, but the other western schools have gone quiet). Maritime institutions pushed for recognition of the unique situation in that region. There were great debates, strongly influenced by university academics, about national social programs, regional economic development, social policy, and the like. These were passionate and even exciting times for a country that seems to recoil from both passion and excitement.

There are few such debates these days. Perhaps in the 1970s they were simply reflecting the zeitgeist. The energy and ideas may have come as much from the public as from the institutions. It is interesting that the continued growth of the university system has not resulted in a burst of citizenship and engagement, has not produced a flood of ideas on how to improve and develop Canada. Instead, the universities have become solid contributors to the economic development of the country, rather than focal points for debates about Canada's future. Perhaps—and this is being nostalgic and wistful—Canadians expected more from the expansion of our universities. It says a lot about the changing nature of our country that a growth spurt launched out of enthusiasm for change has resulted in a system that is comfortable maintaining the status quo.

26 Medical Students Are Getting a Free Ride

Every year, medical doctors educated in Canada leave for the United States. The number spiked in the mid-1990s, when about five hundred left, though it's less than that now. Some do come back though, and in 2006, about sixty more returned than left. Over time, however, more than 10 per cent of doctors trained here have ended up in the United States.

Whatever the number, it costs close to half-a-million dollars to train a doctor, most of which is paid by the taxpayer, and the doctors' leaving amounts to a considerable financial loss to Canada, to say nothing of the fact that our aging population needs all the doctors we can get.

What's the solution? We could waive tuition for doctors who agree to practice in Canada, especially in small or remote communities, for a number of years after graduation. This is the principle on which the military colleges operate—their students must serve a period in the armed forces as the price of their education. Or we could make medical students sign a contract promising to pay the entire cost of their education if they leave the country within a certain period after graduation. Governments are already trying to persuade doctors to practice in rural areas—Liberal leader Michael Ignatieff announced a proposal along these lines in the summer of 2010.

None of this is likely to happen though, mostly because there's a huge element of hypocrisy involved in complaining about the situation. We are guilty too, for we do to the Philippines, South Africa, and other countries the same thing that the United States does to us—we poach their doctors. If it hadn't been for doctors fleeing South Africa in the 1990s, large sections of Saskatchewan, for example, would have been virtually doctorless. In 2006, 22 per cent of doctors practising in Canada were trained in foreign countries, most of which are poorer than we are. So we can't really complain: what's sauce for the goose...

27 Toronto Rules the Canadian Academic World

Canadians love to hate Toronto. They cheer when the Maple Leafs flounder—as they always do. They find secret pleasure when snowstorms bring "Hogtown" to a halt and find schadenfreude in the unending traffic jams on Highway 401. But in the university world, the power of the Greater Toronto Area and, particularly, the larger metropolitan area, cannot be ignored.

The concentration of academic power in the GTA (and nearby in southern Ontario) is something to behold. The University of Toronto, Canada's largest (70,000 students at all campuses), and one of the best public universities in the world, dominates the system. The president of U of T has great access to federal and provincial governments, donors, and decision-makers. Its two satellite campuses—Scarborough and Mississauga—are growing quickly. Other institutions are only an hour or two away (or would be if all the other cars would get off the road).

York University, often controversial and, with 50,000 students, Canada's second-largest English university (the Université de Montréal has 55,000), also has a French-language campus in the city. Within a three-hour drive lie Guelph, McMaster, Brock, Waterloo, Wilfrid Laurier, Western Ontario, Trent, and Queen's. Three of Canada's newest universities—Ryerson, Ontario College of Arts and Design University, and University of Ontario Institute of Technology—are in the GTA.

Two things stand out. First, the institutions listed above have close to 300,000 students—between a quarter and a third of all Canadian university students. No other part of Canada can match the scale, quality, and impact of the GTA institutions. Montreal comes the closest and has one of the highest students-per-1,000 people ratios in North America, but the collective impact tracks well behind Toronto's. To the extent that universities drive national prosperity, Toronto has a huge advantage over all other areas.

Second, and more ominous, the GTA is far and away the largest source of future students in Canada. The metro region believes that it is short some 75,000 spaces—more than the number of university students in Nova Scotia—and there is enormous pressure to open new campuses or brand-new institutions.

For the foreseeable future Toronto will continue to dominate the Canadian university landscape. Indeed, the concentration of academic power in the GTA is probably greater than the city's corporate authority, which has been sliding slowly towards the West. Academically—hard as it is for some of us to accept—Toronto is the centre of the Canadian academic universe. Hogtown rules.

 ## Sports Rule

We (the authors) agree on many subjects, but there are two on which we cannot see eye to eye. The first is the place of athletics at Canadian universities. Our differences seem irreconcilable, so we offer both positions, one here and the other in Chapter 28, and invite readers to make their own choices.

On the one hand...

One of the several ways that United States universities march to the sound of a different drummer is the matter of intervarsity athletics. The multi-billion-dollar, television-enriched, hypercompetitive extravaganza that is American college sports has no counterpart anywhere else in the world.

Intervarsity sports in Canada are not like this. A few basketball teams pack in the fans. A game at Bishop's or St. Francis Xavier is a wonderful community experience. Sitting on metal stands at a Saskatoon Huskies football game is to understand why Saskatchewan is such a great place and what Prairie pride is all about. But compare this to the 80,000 fans jammed into a U.S. college football game or the thousands of "Cameron Crazies" (Duke university sports fanatics) camped out for days to grab a ticket to a Duke versus North Carolina basketball game, and you will realize that Canada plays minor league.

The vast majority of Canadian intervarsity athletics—and the athletes and coaches—represent the ideal of classical sport: participation for the love of it and the chance to push oneself to excel. Many players have to cover some of their own expenses for competing and live with poor facilities, part-time coaches, and very little attention. Coaches accept pitiful stipends and put in hundreds of hours to support their athletes. Crowds rarely extend beyond family members and girl/boyfriends, and the events are mostly ignored by the press. There is honour, blood, sweat, and tears, but little glory in the life of the Canadian student athlete.

Universities can and should build their campus life around recreational and intervarsity athletics. Cheering for the campus team against cross-province rivals is great fun. The student athletes—provided they are both students as well as athletes—are superb ambassadors and great community-builders. The melding of body, mind, and spirit has been a goal of humanity for centuries—check out the bios of Canada's astronauts if you have any doubts—and should be a central feature of campus life. Canadian campuses have too little in the way of athletics and too little sport as part of campus life. Game time!

29 Our Universities Are Eurocentric

Students of non-European ancestry dominate many of the largest university campuses in Canada. Many of their families, particularly those from Asia, place a high premium on a university education—something long unattainable in many countries—and urge their children to succeed academically and gain admittance to the best schools and the best programs. When they come to Canadian campuses, however, they often encounter institutions still firmly rooted in Europe and with surprisingly little coverage of the rest of the world. Universities are supposed to be "universal," awakening in their students an awareness of the human condition. They do, but with a decided emphasis on Europe and European legacy countries such as Canada, the United States, and a few overseas colonies.

Decades ago, universities saw themselves as national cheerleaders. They were responsible for ensuring that students were deeply versed in their national history and traditions. Canada was no different in this regard, and our universities placed a great deal of emphasis on their European antecedents. Over time, this resulted in the development of European coverage in the core social science and humanities disciplines, and a surprisingly limited attention to the rest of the world. Universities were a reflection of the European-based societies from which they came.

Then Canada changed. Massive immigration from East Asia, South Asia, the Caribbean, the Middle East, and Africa altered and enriched the Canadian social fabric. But our institutions shifted only marginally. During the Cold War, Russia got a great deal more attention, and faculty members were hired to study it. When Japan seemed destined to take over as the world's leading economic power, Japan studies grew substantially. And when China replaced Japan as the country of concern, resources shifted to Chinese topics. The ongoing crises in the Middle East and throughout the Islamic world have convinced some institutions to move slowly in this direction. Africa and Latin America, in contrast, have attracted very little attention.

Canadian students of non-European backgrounds can find some coverage of their ancestral homelands, but nothing compared to the resources devoted to European affairs. Many departments would be delighted to expand into new geographical and cultural fields if they were to get additional funding to do so, but are much more reluctant if they have to eliminate European or North American slots.

Equally, Canadian students of European backgrounds have a limited understanding of global affairs because they have few opportunities to take courses outside the Europe–North America zone. And these students are particularly reluctant to study Asian languages, despite the continuing importance of that part of the world. What's more, few programs require students to take specific courses designed to provide a broad understanding of global affairs and to come to terms with developments in emerging or crisis-filled areas.

Canadian universities must take deliberate and thoughtful steps to catch up with globalization and the rapid developments in the non-European world. It's vital that philosophy students be introduced to philosophical thought from East and South Asian countries, that African political cultures be explained to political science students, that English students be exposed to voices outside the Western canon, and that history students understand how Latin America and the Middle East factor into world affairs. Europe and North America will remain important to Canadian students and will even retain their prominent position. But universities let their students down if they do not make concerted and deliberate steps to shift resources to cover other parts of the world.

 ## Engineers Are a Hot-Ticket Item

And they have been since the 1950s and the Cold War space race that sparked the great expansion of the university system. The digital revolution and the search for clean-tech solutions to environmental challenges are only two of the many fields where there's a big demand for engineers.

Companies are anxious to hire engineering co-op students and graduates. Those in the top fields—systems design and software engineering are very popular right now—have little difficulty finding work. And as the global science-based economy ramps up—fuelled by the belief that science- and technology-based innovation holds the key to national prosperity—the need for more engineers will continue to escalate.

Engineers have done well over the past sixty years, but never more so than now. Universities will be hard pressed to keep up with the demand, and the supply of qualified and motivated Canadian students is way too low. If assumptions about a link between national wealth and engineering degrees are true, then the country has some catching up to do.

Forty years ago Canada and other Western nations needed well-trained people, particularly from the social sciences and humanities, to run the large national companies, the multinationals, and rapidly growing governments. The need for engineers was offset by an equal need for a different professional class. Years of streamlining, downsizing, and outsourcing appear to have lessened the appetite for the well-trained generalist in favour of the highly skilled technical person. Universities have not caught up with the transition.

Neither Canada nor the United States is producing enough engineering undergraduates to meet demand. China, India, South Korea, and other Asian nations are doing much better. The vast majority of PhD candidates in engineering are from other countries. Some stay in Canada and the United States and make great contributions; a growing number return to the economic powerhouses of Asia, where there is great demand for their services.

Canadian schools and universities must do better at attracting senior students to careers in engineering. Other countries have gained a real advantage in the engineering sweepstakes—and a significant portion of Canada's prosperity may be at stake.

Business and the University

Business is playing an ever-larger role in Canadian universities. On balance, this is a good and important development. More university training is focused on business-related skills and less on general education. Government grants often require matching funds from business. Successful business leaders have made huge contributions to the top universities, allowing for major expansions in facilities and programming.

Critics have raised legitimate questions about the role of corporations and business leaders in shaping the academic agendas of the campus, accusing them of trying to transform the educational and research functions into feeders for corporations. Business people can be demanding and they often misunderstand the nature and purpose of a university, so the relationships can be very awkward and often tense.

For the past two generations, however, universities have presented themselves as engines of economic development and regional stability. The arguments for major research grants, research facilities, more graduate spots, new programs, and the like are routinely wrapped in promises to enhance training, commercialization, and economic development. These are not new arguments, but they have become more urgent and commonplace in the science-driven innovation economies of the twenty-first century. Students have certainly picked up on the message, and many see a university education as a stepping-stone to prosperity.

Business, government, students, and the general public expect their universities to serve society, and, given that the present generation sees this largely in terms of business development and job creation, universities have little choice but to stay engaged.

That's not to say the entire academic enterprise must be turned over to a corporate agenda. Universities also exist as the analysts, critics, and conscience of society. Canada needs more of the critical and provocative assessment of business and the commercial thrust of the modern age. Most of this critique is currently coming from off campus. Working with business does not mean kowtowing to it.

What does it mean to co-operate with corporations? It means paying close attention to employment market needs and adjusting courses and programs to stay current. It means talking to business leaders to discover opportunities for collaborative research and collective problem-solving. It means expecting Canadian corporations to pay for their share of the research infrastructure and educational enterprise—universities must not become taxpayer-subsidized supports for business.

In turn, the business community has to pay closer attention to the critiques and analysis offered by university, to respond to the moral imperatives of our age, and to commit itself to solving shared problems.

Universities will not lose their autonomy and independence if they co-operate with the corporate sector and engage with it as serious players in the educational and research enterprises. They will instead maintain relevance, attract more resources, better serve their students, and contribute to the economic development of the country if and when they help businesses succeed.

Canadian universities and corporations do not co-operate particularly well. The places that set the gold standard for collaboration—Silicon Valley, the Boston corridor, Finland, South Korea, Singapore, Taiwan, Hong Kong—do much better. That co-operation is fuelling regional competitiveness and employment. These areas get more money from both the corporate world and government, largely because they are contributing to prosperity. There is a lesson to be learned here, and our universities should learn it.

Do Grade 2 Teachers Need Five Years of Post-secondary Education?

Arguably they don't, but there's more to the issue than this. The education of elementary school teachers is a good example of how universities have been used to raise the professional status of certain occupations.

Readers over the age of sixty will remember the day when most elementary school teachers were women. Regulations differed in each province, but the common requirement for these teachers was high school graduation and one year in Teachers' College. These young teachers could begin a career in their late teens.

It's easy to understand why high school teachers need a university degree (and they usually have one). A Grade 12 physics teacher certainly should have a good training in physics (though not all of them do). But why does a Grade 2 teacher need a degree in anything? Surely the first requirement for a teacher at that level is a love of children, and that can't be learned.

But these teachers of the past, often admired and romanticized, were exploited. Because of their short training period, and because the majority were women and non-unionized, salaries were very low and pensions tiny. This, and not necessarily any love of the job, was why many teachers taught for forty-five years, hoping their savings would last after they were forcibly retired at sixty-five.

The road to professionalization began in the 1950s, with unionization and collective bargaining. Higher salaries meant that more men chose to be elementary teachers, and this in turn led to a stronger union. One way to boost the status and pay of teaching was to push for higher academic requirements, a drive that coincided with the government's wish to have a more highly educated population.

And so, in the 1960s, the provinces began to require elementary teachers to have Bachelor's degrees. The requirement was not retroactive, but since their salaries depended on their level of education, all but the oldest began to take extension courses to complete a degree. The next step was the Master of Education degree, which put teachers in an even higher salary bracket (the current difference between the salary of a teacher with four years' education and one with six, at the top rank, can be as much as $15,000). A Master's degree in science or arts would have had the same effect, but hardly any teachers took these degrees.

Nowadays education requirements for teachers vary widely across Canada. In some provinces, three undergraduate years plus a year of teacher training is the minimum; in others it's four years plus one or even two years of teacher training. Some have an "integrated" degree, where teaching and other requirements are completed in four years. Add the MEd—which usually comes later after some time in the classroom—and the total can range from four to six or even seven years—the same as a doctor, and more than a lawyer.

Sure, teaching is a tough job that requires a high level of skill, but does a four-year arts degree with a major in English, followed by a year of teacher training, impart this skill? It's hard to think that a Grade 2 teacher needs as much training as a physician does, and the logical explanation is simply the urge to professionalize what used to be a respected but ill-paid job. Teachers have accomplished this brilliantly. Whether it benefits the students or the general public is a different matter.

 # The Science Tsunami

It may seem extraordinary, but four out of five of all the scientists who ever worked are alive today. Think about that number, and think about all the stuff they are churning out. As late as the 1950s, science was a small field, occupied by researchers working on fairly broad and fundamental problems. Now research work has increasingly been split into small and esoteric inquiries. The total volume of research output overwhelms anyone attempting to stay abreast of new developments. We are staring a scientific tsunami in the face.

It will be magnified by the rapid growth of scientific work in China, India, and eventually the Middle East and Africa. The world is already awash in research papers, grant applications, new theories and ideas, and laboratories. What will it be like in twenty years, when scientific output has doubled and doubled again?

This flood of science hides some brilliant, life-changing work, some potentially dangerous discoveries, a great deal of career-building activity, and a tiny amount of bogus and fraudulent nonsense. How do we tell good from bad, useful from dangerous, legitimate from garbage? Commonly, science runs well ahead of legal and moral concerns, as with the use of gender-based abortions to remove female fetuses, new forms of genetic testing, and the misuse of computer science discoveries by criminals.

The scientists we work with are dedicated scholars, as devoted to their studies as historians and literary researchers are to theirs. Quite a lot of their work fails any real test of relevance and practicality (just like the humanities), but the scientific community has nonetheless done a great deal to convince governments that their work is worthy of more and continuing support.

It's true, the world needs more science, but it needs even more scientific understanding. The explosion of research has overwhelmed our capacity to know and understand what is coming out of the laboratories and field research. The world needs more scientific communicators, more practitioners of the scholarship of synthesis.

We need more people who can wade through the piles of research papers to find the gems that truly illuminate and the trends that can change our lives. We need more awareness of science, more understanding of the impact of new discoveries. And we need, perhaps, less of the original laboratory work that already vastly outstrips our collective capacity to understand and to use effectively.

The new scientist will be a well-trained generalist, able to sift through scientific debris to find the occasional gem, and determined to share the best discoveries with the public, government, and industry. Scientific research must continue, for much depends on improving our understanding of the world. But we need a new type of scientist to save us from drowning in the scientific deluge.

The Public Doesn't Get Academic Research

Frantz Fanon wouldn't get a Social Sciences and Humanities Research Council grant, and Thomas Edison would be turned down for a Natural Sciences and Engineering Research Council award. So, at least, goes the mantra of critics of academic research.

The Tri-Council agencies and their close partner, the Canada Foundation for Innovation, sponsor millions of dollars-worth of research each year, supporting faculty members in curiosity-based research programs with one of the best-funded and most academically sound granting arrangements in the world. Those less fond of the system argue it is tilted towards careerist and disciplinary pursuits and is not well suited to supporting problem-solving and the general interests of the public at large.

Is the charge fair? Frantz Fanon, a psychiatrist from Martinique, published on the colonial experience from the perspective of the colonized peoples. His books—more argument and even polemic than well-researched analysis—sold many copies, sparked intellectual and political ferment throughout the developing world, and revolutionized world politics in the process. Edison, among the most practical and successful inventors of all time, introduced radical technological changes, backed by strong commercial applications. He would have been the poster child for innovation strategies had he lived in the twenty-first century, but his experimental approaches were more hit-and-miss than systematic—"99 per cent perspiration, 1 per cent inspiration." These people, and many others, were able to generate ideas, innovations, and inventions of enormous importance without help from any university.

This sort of thing still happens. Private companies—the Xerox Laboratory is a prime example, but Canadian firms such as Research In Motion, Open Text, and (before its disastrous fall) Nortel—have also produced great original research. And non-academic think-tanks continue to produce useful commentaries, like those supported in Canada by the Fraser Institute, the North-South Institute, the Centre for International Governance Innovation, the Canada West Foundation, Public Policy Forum, and the C.D. Howe Institute. So—the argument goes—solid, practical, relevant work can be done outside the academy. Why then bother with all of the funding for mainstream academic work?

Having received Tri-Council funding on several occasions, it would be hypocritical for us to turn on agencies that have supported us, and thousands of other Canadian researchers, over the years. We have no desire to do so in any case. In the heyday of government-sponsored research funding—the 1970s and 1980s—the system really was curiosity-driven and faculty-focused. But then the academy heard mounting complaints about "irrelevant" scholarship—the Reform Party of Canada used to routinely try to embarrass the government by publicizing seemingly frivolous research grants—and adjusted accordingly.

The Social Sciences and Humanities Research Council faced the toughest road, largely because funding was so short (fewer than 30 per cent of applicants receive funding in the regular competitions). The Natural Sciences and Engineering Research Council and the Canadian Institutes of Health Research made the transition more readily, partly because there's less public criticism of science and technology than of the arts. It's hard for the average person on the street to complain about a complex project on string theory, but easy to pontificate about the folly of spending tax dollars on studies of "Wartime Shakespeare in a Global Context," "Things in the Mind: Cognitive Psychology in the Later Middle Ages," or "Manuscripts and the Forms of Middle English Literary Texts," to pick three examples at random from the 2009 awards.

All the funding agencies, however, have adjusted their programs to include greater community engagement—more partnerships with business, government agencies, and community groups, and a strong emphasis on sharing research results with the public. Research relationships with indigenous groups have been turned on their head to ensure a greater and more constructive impact on Aboriginal communities.

Universities never claimed to be the only places where new ideas would be generated. They never claimed that all research should be handled on campuses. Indeed, universities have routinely embraced radical, creative, and innovative thinkers from outside the academy. The writings and discoveries of non-academics routinely show up on academic reading lists. Academic research is deliberately different from the free-flowing, open-ended exchange of ideas and insights that occurs in free and democratic societies. Scholars test ideas and concepts, follow clearly articulated and reproducible methods, and subject their results to rigorous peer review before publication, with the expectation that their work will stand the test of time.

A robust and open society takes its ideas and innovation wherever they are found. Academics are a substantial part of the research puzzle, producing original ideas, testing concepts, improving upon and refining ideas, and exploring new ways of knowing and explaining the natural and human worlds. But they share the public space with many others, from journalists to government agents, researchers in think-tanks, and members of the general public. Fanon, Edison, and many others changed the world for the better—as did countless university researchers who used their institutional base to both address relevant and time-sensitive questions and to explore topics derived from their imagination.

IV
Do Canadian Universities Work?

35   Putting Bums On Seats Is the Number-One Priority

Over the last thirty years, two forces have combined to cause a crisis for many universities. First, in many parts of the country the number of high school students levelled off and then declined. Second, it turned out that not every student who graduated from high school *wanted* to go to university.

In the Maritime provinces there were not enough students to stock the region's many universities—which include some of the country's finest and most attractive institutions. Meanwhile, in Alberta, high school graduates weighed the prospect of four years of study against the high wages of the oil patch. The choice between thirty dollars an hour and Derrida turned out to be a no-brainer for many eighteen-year-olds, and quite often they chose construction over deconstruction.

What's more, even if the young choose differently, the demographics are alarming for universities: in Saskatchewan and Manitoba the number of high school graduates is declining rapidly, as it is in most of Ontario outside the Greater Toronto Area, and in much of British Columbia outside the lower mainland. Put simply, the flow of well-trained and highly motivated high school graduates is slowing at a time when universities need steady or expanding numbers to meet their always-rising costs.

These realities have created a serious challenge, with universities launching aggressive marketing campaigns to attract students—increasingly *any* students—to come to campus.

Universities desperate for warm bodies have had no choice but to go down the grade scale, even though they all know that these students are at academic risk from the beginning. Research has shown consistently that students who are below average (in Ontario, 80 per cent now) in their high school studies face serious difficulties in university. But universities need full classrooms to pay the bills. At least one university (Brandon) will admit any person with a high school diploma—period. And if that standard proves too high, applicants can wait until they are twenty-one years old and then qualify as mature students.

Knowing that university was within relatively easy grasp was not always good enough for many students and parents. They wanted—and demanded—access to a university education close to home. This is why the Greater Toronto Area has a stunning shortage of university spaces, predicted to reach 75,000 within the next few years. Ontario has plenty of extra spots, in Thunder Bay, Windsor, St. Catharines, Brantford, North Bay—all homes to respectable universities. But the pressure on the government to expand opportunities close to home has put pressure on York and Toronto to develop feeder campuses, convinced Trent to open a facility in downtown Toronto, has Milton negotiating with Wilfrid Laurier University on the development of a new campus, and convinced Lakehead to open a branch in Orillia.

But think of this nationally for a second. Stellar universities—Bishop's, St. Francis Xavier, Mount Allison, and Acadia—are desperate for students and would happily take in hundreds from the GTA. So would Lakehead, Nipissing, Brandon, Regina, Saskatchewan, and Manitoba. But instead of working as a national network, and moving students to where the spaces are to be found, governments understand the imperative of the new post-secondary order: parents and students demand a spot close to home.

And so the Canadian university system is expanding in a few places and contracting or struggling in others. The Toronto universities are bursting at the seams, and campuses within relatively easy commuting distance are attracting a sizeable overflow. Alberta is taking up the slack through four-year degree programs at Mount Royal College in Calgary and Grant McEwan College in Edmonton. British Columbia has converted urban university colleges (Malaspina, Kwantlen, Fraser Valley, Emily Carr) to university status (Vancouver Island University, Kwantlen Polytechnic University, University of the Fraser Valley, Emily Carr University of Art + Design). At the other extreme, places such as Memorial's Cornerbrook campus, the University of New Brunswick at Saint John and St. Thomas in New Brunswick, UPEI on Prince Edward Island, the smaller University of Quebec campuses, Winnipeg, Brandon, Regina, UNBC, and the like struggle to attract enough students to meet their needs.

Even if they can come up with the right number of first-year students, many of these institutions are admitting significant numbers with very low likelihood of succeeding. This situation will only worsen in the coming years, as the numbers of high school graduates in outlying regions continue to fall and as their cohort in key urban centres continues to grow.

The end result of all this is that recruiting has emerged as a growth industry in Canada. Universities and specialized programs now spend hundreds of thousands of dollars wooing students (and their parents) and trying to influence guidance counsellors. Large university and college fairs are held in major centres. Recruiters visit virtually every high school of substantial size in the country. The elite schools make special visits to selected high schools—"selected" being a euphemism for institutions with lots of wealthy and well-educated young people. Private schools are particularly attractive recruiting grounds. Schools in working-class districts or immigrant settlement areas rarely get the same attention. Firms like the Canadian recruitment company EZRecruit use new technologies to personalize university pamphlets and to provide "personal" contact between the university and students.

How can universities avoid this crisis? The federal and provincial governments, supported by private donors, could step in with special travel awards to cover the additional costs of attending university out of province—but this would probably have little effect. It's more likely that, in the next ten years or so, some universities will be forced to close or to dramatically restructure themselves. This is already occurring in elementary and high schools, and universities will be next.

Change is certainly on the horizon. Some freestanding institutions will likely be merged into a provincial or regional university system, if only to save administrative costs. Some will change from degree-granting status to serving as local access points for first- and second-year students only. Others, seeking to stay independent and relevant, will drop their claims to comprehensiveness and switch to serve specialized academic and professional markets. This, in fact, is the most positive and logical outcome. But since it likely entails adopting a polytechnic approach to post-secondary education—merging university and college programming—it will be fought bitterly by faculty, students, and the institutions at large.

Strong, deliberate action is required, but we're more likely to see a process of grudging, step-by-step change, a process that will only add to the costs, time, and difficulty of aligning Canada's post-secondary resources with the needs, aspirations, and requirements of the country.

The Perils of Athletics

On the other hand...

You can also argue that athletics have the potential to seriously corrupt universities, though happily there are as yet no campus statues to university football coaches in Canada.

It really depends on what kind of athletics you are talking about. There's no doubt that participation in sports for the sake of sport can be character-building. No one objects to a university's sponsoring a volleyball, fencing, track, swimming, or other team, or to the major sports—football, basketball, hockey—played intramurally.

The problem arises with the major intervarsity sports—that is, the major sports played between universities. These are the ones that people want to watch, and they are the expensive ones. With this importance comes the possibility of corruption.

Think of the many ways university athletics can be corrupted. A favoured athlete can be offered a summer sinecure by a businessman who is a fan of the team. Money can be funnelled to star athletes in various ways: part-time non-jobs, gifts, the loan of a car, and so on. The Canadian Interuniversity Athletic Union has strict rules designed to prevent the corruption of sport in this way, but it's tough to keep it clean.

Athletics is treading on dangerous ground when a game or a team play-ing a major sport becomes symbolic of a university, when competition becomes a matter of prestige, when fans and alumni chime in to demand victory. Then corners can be cut and rules broken, and the athletes come under tremendous pressure (some of it self-generated). Result: situations like the 2010 steroid scandal involving members of the University of Waterloo football team, or even more horribly, the dreadful Sandusky sex abuse case at Penn State, which happened not because athletes and coaches are particularly prone to such things, but because the football program was so worshipped that no one paid attention to the rumours of what was going on. It's hard to imagine the Penn State disaster happening here, because Canadians do not blindly adore their athletic programs, but, still, it's a black mark on the concept of university athletics.

Perhaps the most corrupting way in which athletics affect universities is that they create, or can create, a group of non-student athletes, people (almost always men, because traditionally it's the men's teams that really matter) who come to university only to play sports, and who fake their courses as much as they can. Universities that offer degrees in education, particularly physical education, can (not all do) offer practical courses that anyone can pass. A few top grades in such courses can offset failures in heavier courses, keeping the athlete's grade above 60 per cent, enabling him to stay eligible for intercollegiate athletics for several years. At the end of this, if he drops out without a degree, no one much cares. He's served his purpose.

Why Canadian universities permit this to happen is a mystery. It's different in the United States, where huge sums of money are at stake. An American university team that wins the March Madness national basketball championship can receive millions of extra dollars in alumni donations. This doesn't happen in Canada, where alumni are less generous. When Canadian universities give away their integrity, they do it for free. Fortunately, serious scandals don't happen very often, but the only real preventative is not to have intervarsity athletics at all.

University Education Should Be Co-ordinated Nationally

Can anything be done to prevent universities' closing? There is one solution, but it will test the capacity of Canadian institutions to collaborate and the ability of provincial systems to operate in the national interest.

There are just too many spaces in some parts of the country and not enough in others. Ontario is feverishly adding thousands more—20,000 college and university spots in 2010 alone, or more than the capacity of the entire New Brunswick university system. In 2012, the Ontario government announced a plan to add 40,000 new spaces on three new campuses in the Greater Toronto Area. British Columbia has created thousands of new spaces in the lower mainland, and Alberta created spaces largely by converting community colleges to universities.

The solution is simple. We must deflect applications from overcrowded universities to those with space. Stop adding capacity in the big cities and direct students to unused spots in other areas. Provide a little money towards travel costs. Publicize the opportunities across the country. Ensure guidance counsellors advise students of the full range of educational options in Canada. If an Ontario student, university eligible, applies to Toronto, Queen's, and Western, and fails to make the cut, offer her a spot at Nipissing or Windsor. Even better, encourage her to consider universities in another province.

Here's how it would work. Instead of receiving three rejections, she gets a letter listing all the Canadian universities willing to accept her, which are then free to contact her. The pain of being turned down by her first choices is alleviated when she is courted by several attractive universities she hadn't considered. A student who applied to UBC, Victoria, and Simon Fraser ends up at the University of Saskatchewan. Another from Mississauga enrolls at St. Mary's in Halifax. A third, unable to get into the University of Alberta, Lethbridge, or Calgary, opts to attend Memorial University of Newfoundland. They all discover different parts of the country and get the education they want.

But don't hold your breath. Canadian students do not like to leave home and—for reasons of finances and family bonds—many parents are not happy to see them go, at least at this stage of their lives. Even worse, an exercise like this would require an unprecedented level of inter-provincial co-operation. Have we seen much of this lately? Alas, an excellent chance to match student demand with university supply probably will not happen. Without the national will to operate our universities as a federal system the inevitable will happen—sooner or later, some Canadian universities are going to close.

38 Governing the University

Having university senates has been compared to "letting the lunatics run the asylum." It's a common cliché that reflects the general view of academic governance. Is it fair? Only partly.

Universities have two governing bodies (sometimes with different names): a board of governors and a senate. The first controls financial, property, and similar issues, and is ultimately responsible for the well-being of the university. The second controls academic matters.

The board of governors is a mix of appointees (often by government) and elected faculty, student, and staff representatives. The senate is controlled by elected faculty members, with significant student representation, and is responsible for making all the key academic decisions: program approvals and changes, entrance requirements, academic penalties, schedules, examination rules, and on and on. Senates have many committees and sub-committees that award scholarships and honorary degrees, hear student appeals, act as disciplinary tribunals, and carry out many other duties. Joint board/senate committees serve as hiring committees for new presidents and senior administrators.

Senates can provide sound academic advice. They review programs for rigour and intellectual substance. They attend to accreditation requirements and strive to ensure cultural and theoretical breadth. They hold the administration's feet to the fire—usually in a collegial and co-operative way. They set, in other words, the intellectual standards and culture for the entire university. Senate debates can be vigorous and sometimes nasty, but they can also be useful. Universities must have senates, and a constructive and able senate can do much to enhance the quality of the institution and the student experience.

But senates can also be ineffective and can slow the work of the university. They can be dominated by people with an axe to grind—particularly faculty unions or students focused on a small number of issues. They often move very slowly and unproductively, devoting huge amounts of time and paper to minor academic administrative matters. At their worst they become battlegrounds between faculty and the administration, straying off academic and into management issues. The amount of high-quality debate about truly academic issues is generally small. The committee structure can be overwhelming: to change the requirements for a course in sociology, for example, the change must be approved by the sociology department (and maybe a curriculum subcommittee too), an arts faculty council, the curriculum committee of the senate, and finally by the whole senate. That's a lot of time spent by highly educated people to decide a simple matter.

Senates need to be reformed rather than eliminated. They vary widely in quality and effectiveness from institution to institution, often reflecting the respect given to the body by the administration and vice versa. A more specific mandate—focusing on high-level issues such as medium- and long-term planning, new programs, campus life, and the like—would be useful, with more detailed matters delegated to other levels of the collegial process. The committee structure needs to be streamlined.

Senates should be learning bodies, where the university discusses and debates its place within the region, nation, and world. There are many forces swirling around universities—commercialization of research, role of private donors, demographic change, and the shifting expectations of students and parents. University faculty and students have a great deal to contribute to the understanding of how these influences will affect universities. Senates should be the embodiment of the intellectual and research-based contributions of the academy.

Want to focus attention on this issue? Put a cost on the operation of these systems—in faculty and staff time for preparation and meetings—and then decide if the shockingly high expenditure is worth the money.

39 The Three-Year Degree

Have you ever wondered why university courses run twelve or thirteen weeks in Canada? Or why degree programs usually require five courses a semester for four years, or forty courses, to complete the degree? And how did we settle on the three hours per week standard for most lecture courses (science classes are different). This is the Canadian and American standard, though there is some local variation. The answer is mostly that this is the way it's always been done. In universities, traditions are very powerful, and we think that this is a good one.

Over the decades, the university system has settled on four years as the standard for an undergraduate degree. Three-year degrees are still around, but they represent a lesser academic or professional accomplishment. This is an odd quirk in the academic system, effectively conferring the same degree for significantly less time, effort and investment. Sometimes they are called "pass" degrees, but this is not always made clear on the certificate.

The three-year degree represents one full year less study, ten fewer courses, and usually a lot less effort (in many programs, students don't have to declare a major; that is, concentrate on a field). After graduation there is no requirement that they identify their degree as the result of a three-year program instead of the standard four-year undertaking. As a consequence, holders of this shorter degree are competing in the marketplace with those who worked for the full four years.

There have been some really substandard three-year degrees offered. Until recently, Brandon University offered a three-year degree called the Bachelor of General Studies, which permitted students to take any courses they liked for three years. The idea was to let them craft their own programs, with the thought that someone really keen on Anthropology, for example, might take every course the Anthropology department offered, something that the usual programs did not permit. What happened instead was that most people in the BGS program took the easiest courses they could find, with emphasis on first-year courses, and it was particularly popular with student athletes. It wasn't much of a degree, but at least it had a different name.

Argue the matter as you will, it is undeniable that a three-year degree is a significantly lesser accomplishment than a four-year degree. Three-year graduates study less, learn less, work less and, logically, know less. They have settled for a second-tier degree, for whatever reasons. No one considers a three-quarter marathon to be the same as a real marathon, but for some reason the three-year designation shows remarkable staying power.

So why do universities offer it? In part, because there is a demand for it. The three-year degree has been attractive to part-time, mature, and distance-education students because it allows faster completion for what is already a long and drawn-out process. It is an alternate exit for students struggling to finish their studies. For those with a few failed classes and with interest flagging, the three-year degree offers an exit with dignity. The three-year degree is also attractive to some very talented students. Some of the country's law, medicine, pharmacy, and other programs admit exceptional applicants without a full degree. In such situations, the students can opt for a three-year degree and then continue their studies at the professional level.

Despite the fact that it represents significantly less substance, the three-year degree attracts thousands of students per year. The gap between the three- and four-year degree attracts little public comment and seems to be an awkward secret the universities like to keep to themselves.

In this context, Ontario government's interest in expanding the three-year degree offering makes no sense except as a money-saving device, which is presumably the reason the province is promoting it. Given the importance attached to higher education, it is illogical that the government would support the expansion of a clearly inferior degree designation. In fact, it is a sign of accessibility and credential madness, as well as a sign of Ontario's budget problems. Wouldn't it be nice if all undergraduates finished in three years? Think of the savings if thousands of students finished in three years instead of four.

Over the past decade, several provinces have insisted that students stay in high school until they graduate or are eighteen years of age. The stated purpose was to increase high school graduation rates. The goal was achieved, but with the effect of keeping thousands of unmotivated and disengaged students in school. To accommodate these academically disinclined students, the school systems had to create some lesser high school credentials for them, or some alternate paths to a diploma. The politicians got to brag about improved graduation rates while teachers struggled to teach students whose only wish was to escape their classes.

The Ontario proposal for more three-year degrees makes sense in this context. Having created a high school system where almost everyone gets to graduate—an outcome that is supposedly good for students' self-esteem—they now seem to want a university system where everyone gets in and gets out with a degree as soon as academic decency permits. The Ontario colleges, always anxious to expand into the field of university offerings, say they would be happy to give the degrees.

Ontario's plan is wrong-headed. If, according to longstanding North American tradition, a degree is four years in length, then this should be the standard. If universities (or governments) want to offer lesser designations, they should do so under another name. Call them Associate Degrees (some universities offer Associate Degrees after two years of studies, which is also misleading). Differentiate between a degree and a partial program of study. Then let the employment market decide, with full truth in advertising.

Universities should be more flexible and creative than they are at present. It is odd, indeed, that the system has played fast and loose with one of the absolutely foundational elements—length of program and study—allowing students, parents, and employers alike to think that 3=4, an absurdity even by the standards of "new Math."

 # Universities and Colleges Are Fighting Tooth and Nail

Universities and colleges in Canada should be natural allies. They have a great deal in common, serve the same governments and public, and play crucial roles in ensuring Canadian competitiveness. But they just don't get along.

The public rarely sees the tensions and difficulties that have slowed innovation in the system for decades. Colleges find universities arrogant, aloof, pretentious, and far too academic (that is, non-practical). Universities see colleges as unscholarly, non-academic (that is, having low standards), overly practical and too concerned with meeting employers' needs. The public and guidance counsellors (most of whom are university graduates) clearly see university degrees as more prestigious than college diplomas. Governments, following the public's lead, favour them. Not many colleges have expensive and architecturally impressive buildings. Pragmatism is the college way.

Universities and colleges can and must collaborate. In many ways, combining university education and college training is ideal. Some students are clearly destined for university; others are best suited for college. But a substantial group would benefit from a combined university-college program.

Many possibilities exist, including two-plus-two arrangements (two years of college and two years of university), college post-graduate certificates and, more rarely, integrated college-university programs (four- or five-year programs producing a diploma and a degree). And some are operating now: Guelph-Humber, McMaster-Mohawk (collaborative Bachelor of Science in Nursing and Bachelor of Technology programs); Seneca-York; nursing programs in Saskatchewan; and several BC collaborations.

Growing rivalries will exacerbate the challenges. In Ontario, some colleges have been authorized to offer degrees. In Alberta, Grant McEwan and Mount Royal have degree-granting authority. British Columbia converted a number of colleges to university-colleges and then to non-research universities (one, Okanagan University College, was split in two, the research part becoming a branch of the University of British Columbia, and the other reverting to the name Okanagan College). Universities, for their part, are shifting to more practical approaches and more employment-focused degrees and diplomas.

College-university collaborations would improve efficiency, career readiness, and responsiveness to market trends in the post-secondary sector. But major movement here is unlikely. Faculty at both universities and colleges will fight it. Institutional autonomy works against effective partnerships, as do the competing cultures of colleges and universities. If only universities would learn to respect the colleges, and the colleges would stop longing to become universities.

The lack of collaboration produces losers and no winners. Students have fewer well-developed study and career options. Governments pay too much for duplicate programs of studies. Employers have trouble getting the workers they want. And the Canadian economy ends up with a widening gap between available jobs and trained and ready workers. It's truly unfortunate that colleges and universities cannot overcome their differences.

Graduate Student Over-production

The number of graduate students in the country has grown by a remarkable 80 per cent since 2000 to more than 195,000. The growth is due, in part, to the credential fever that is sweeping Canada. Thirty years ago, a Bachelor's degree was sufficient to differentiate someone from the rest of the job-seeking crowd. Now, the argument goes, a Master's degree has become the new point of separation. Many students and parents launch into university studies expecting that two degrees will be essential for success. Given the employment and underemployment difficulties faced by Bachelor's degree holders, it is not surprising that many choose to double-down on their career gamble by getting a second degree.

Governments generally fund graduate students more generously than they do undergraduates. The Ontario Graduate Scholarship Program, to give one example, has been going for fifty years now. It pays students $5,000 a semester for up to three years of graduate study, and 3,000 of them are awarded annually. SSHRC and NSERC award graduate scholarships in the Social Sciences/Humanities and the Natural and Physical Sciences. Students can work as Teaching Assistants for a stipend that is decent or stingy, depending on the institution, and there are a number of discipline-specific scholarships, particularly in the sciences. On the whole, many though not all Canadian graduate students are decently funded, particularly at the doctoral level. The number of graduate students per capita, however, is less than in other countries; we are twenty-third place by this standard. Partly for this reason, Ontario, for example, not only doubled the number of gradu-ate spots for domestic students over a four-year period, but gave a $46,000 capital allocation per student to fuel graduate recruiting.

However, at no point does market-place planning appear to have been part of the graduate-student expansion initiatives. While there is great demand for graduate-trained individuals in selected fields—electrical engin-eering, economics, nursing, accounting—no employers are clamouring for a large increase in the number of graduate biologists, historians, or area studies specialists. Universities were left alone to recruit the students where and as they wished.

Universities have recruited successfully, with both master's and doctoral programs increasing across the country. Between 1999 and 2009, doctoral enrolment in Canada increased by 61 per cent, and master's programs by 38 per cent. The figures for Ontario alone were 67 per cent and 51 per cent. (Nationally, 56 per cent of Master's students and 47 per cent of doctoral students were female.)

The results for the students, however, seem mixed. Some of them have had great success in the workplace. In technical fields, opportunities are many and wages high. For those in older disciplinary fields, however, the job market has been largely unfriendly: lots of opportunities for people with an MSc in some engineering fields, not many for those with an MA in English. At the PhD level, graduate expansion has occurred at a time when universities have limited their hiring of tenure-stream faculty members. In some fields, the number of PhDs has gone up three or four times when there are many fewer jobs available. From a workforce-management point of view, this expansion is wrong-headed if not irresponsible. Much the same appears to be the case at the Master's level in traditional academic fields, since government hiring (a primary destination for these degree holders) has been stalled for some time. Not surprisingly, the return on investment for these degrees is minimal, in some fields negative! Professional academics themselves publicly admit that there are far too many PhDs for the number of academic positions available.

MBA programs, seemingly the embodiment of career-readiness, have expanded dramatically, probably to the point of diminishing returns. Athabasca University, for example, has some 1,200 MBA students per year studying online, and Royal Roads University has several successful offerings. Return on investment data shows that students in the elite (and expensive) MBA programs like Rotman, Schulich, HEC, McGill, and UBC do well post-graduation. The direct financial benefits for students in less prestigious MBAs in smaller regional universities do less well.

There is a bright light in the field beyond the MBA. Professional master's degrees, aimed specifically at providing career-ready degrees, are often designed in league with employers. Fees are often much higher (tuition fees for first-year medical students in Canada, for example, range between $12,000 and $20,000, except in Quebec) and students rarely get institutional financial support. These students, however, are highly motivated, career focused and very keen to learn marketable fields. Employers have been drawn to the graduates, in part because of the career orientation and work ethic of the students.

There is a simple message here: professional programs are underdeveloped and due to expand dramatically in the coming years. They are, if nothing else, an overdue response to the over-production of Bachelor's degree holders, providing a second-degree and a career-ready option for disgruntled graduates. The second message is just as simple: traditional disciplinary degrees have grown too fast and too far, attracting many students who are not well-suited for advanced academic study and producing many more graduates than the employment market can possibly bear.

Universities have been remarkably unconcerned about the career experiences of their graduates, and doubly so about the outcomes for their non-professional graduate students. The costs to students and to society as a whole are considerable, and unemployment or underemployment of graduate degree holders only adds to societal dissatisfaction with universities. It is vital, on a national scale, that the country's universities bring the production of disciplinary and professional graduate degrees closer in line with the needs of the Canadian economy.

V

The View from the
Front of the Class

The Good Old Days

The modern university is a big and diverse place, with food courts, campus pubs, and recreation facilities ranging from treadmills to climbing walls. They are multicultural places, with Aboriginal and international students, more women than men, and a bevy of professional schools.

The students of the post-war period had very different campus lives. First, the crush of returning World War II veterans changed the dynamics on campus, which began to grow rapidly, a process that accelerated in the early 1960s as the baby boomers began to arrive. McMaster University, to give as an example one of our alma maters, has expanded fifteen-fold since the war, from fewer than 2,000 students to more than 28,000. Classes were large, though (first-year History at McMaster in 1959 had 300 students), course and program options few, and amenities minimal. These were austere places, and not just because of prohibitions on alcohol on campus, single-gender residences, curfews and other restrictions. Cafeteria food was notoriously bad. To make it worse, professors were aloof and often intimidating. Students did not do written evaluations of their instructors, nor could they defame them online. There was almost no help for students who found course work too hard. It was an era of "root hog, or die," to quote one of our less favourite professors.

If you compare amenities, services, student-centred programming, and many other attributes of the universities of the 1950s with present offerings, the older ones seem like pretty student-unfriendly places. Why, then, are graduates from that era so nostalgic about their experiences and so loyal to their institutions? Part of the answer is what the French call *nostalgie de la boue,* nostalgia for the mud—that is, a yearning for the grubbiness and poverty of the past. As today's students will discover half a century from now, it's almost always better to be young than old. The older institutions, too, had advantages, despite their lack of amenities and their authoritarian nature. First, universities were smaller places, and just as Acadia or Mt. Alison produce a better campus life than the University of Toronto or the University of Alberta, so did the much smaller universities of the 1950s provide a more intimate atmosphere than the large and complex institutions of today.

Secondly, the limited number of course and program options meant that students had many more experiences in common, and there was less angst about course choice, because there was so little of it. By most accounts, students were more actively engaged in campus activities than they are now, and because fewer had to work during the academic year, they had more time for those activities. The relative absence of alcohol on campus meant a greater variety of activities, and less boisterous ones. Few students had cars or much spending money. Campus traditions, from first-year hazing rituals ("initiation," as it was called) to sporting events and inter-faculty contests and social events, featured prominently in students' lives. Sadie Hawkins dances (women did the asking) were common, as were homecoming football games and other intervarsity sports, as well as church services and academic events. McMaster had a "chapel break" every morning, though attendance was not compulsory. There were some—mostly bright students from working-class and low-income backgrounds—who organized work around their studies, but the majority focused their time on their school work. Fifteen hours of class a week and no part time job left many hours for study and recreation. Many students spent their whole academic career in residence, rather than renting off-campus apartments, making the campus their second home.

These students had fun while at university, and they did so with fewer facilities, less money, and less freedom. With smaller campuses, there were better chances to get to know more students and to get to know them well. The campus itself provided distractions and entertainment that students now find in the movie theatre, downtown bars and concert halls, video games and other technological distractions. Most campuses were a lot more monocultural, with fewer barriers of language, culture, and experience between students. Indeed, legendary rivalries between Faculties—Aggies and the Engineers, Engineers and the Arts students—animated university life in ways that they rarely do now.

Canadian universities, with the exception of some of the smaller campuses and some very cohesive Faculties and Departments, particularly of a career-oriented nature, do not generate a comparable level of loyalty, nor do they provide a quality of campus experience like that of the universities of the 1950s and 1960s. In university circles, size does matter, in an inverse way. The alumni from the post-war universities have been loyal to their alma maters and have provided substantial financial, political, and moral support. It is hard to imagine that the mega-versities of the twenty-first century, with their huge classes, large and diverse student bodies, and complicated campus environments, will generate comparable commitment and enthusiasm among graduates down the road. There is a reason Grandma and Grandpa are nostalgic about their university experience. They had fun. They made friends. They spent most of their time on campus. They found the work demanding but not overwhelming, because the higher secondary school standards of that era had prepared them for it.

Universities lose something when they grow, and particularly when they grow beyond a few thousand students. Those who have positive student experiences—and this still applies to many young adults at Canadian universities—are likely to remain connected to and supportive of their alma mater. The growing number of Canadian students who are disengaged from campus life and who do not have a positive social and cultural experience may feel a much weaker connection.

Are the Fine Arts Undervalued?

Over the past fifty years or so, universities have increasingly become more practical places, as the focus on the liberal arts has given way to subjects such as business and the applied and health sciences. Some would say they are too practical, while others would say they are not enough so. Wherever the truth lies, it has been a long time since anyone took seriously the idea that universities are "ivory towers." Through this period, the traditional emphasis on the liberal arts has dimmed, and the Fine and Performing Arts have faced particularly tough times.

Never a career-oriented set of disciplines, or at least not one that promised wealth, the Fine and Performing Arts now seem out of step with the growing emphasis on jobs and income. Indeed, measured by the standard endlessly touted by government—money—graduates in these fields do not do particularly well. The narrow view of the role of the Fine and Performing Arts in the modern university is unfortunate because it fails to take into account the many ways that students in these fields and the campuses as a whole benefit from their presence.

Ironically—and perhaps inevitably—some Fine Arts programs have adopted the language of the market economy, rather than holding to the idea that the Fine and Performing Arts are unique programs, designed for those seeking to explore and develop their creativity. Consider this over-the-top promotional blurb from York University:

> *Many students interested in applying to Theatre are faced with questions from their parents and friends such as: "What will you do with a degree in Theatre?" A degree in Theatre is great preparation for almost any job. You learn how to work independently on a group project, to meet real deadlines, and you learn to see how your part fits into the whole...As a Fine Arts student, you will develop skills that are applicable to many different careers.*

This is misleading. By all the standard economic measures, such as job opportunities and income levels, Fine and Performing Arts graduates do not do well. There are many good reasons to major in Theatre, but money is not one of them.

Still, the Fine and Performing Arts are a valuable asset to campus life. Students, faculty, and staff benefit from the art shows, musical productions, and live theatre that is made possible through active Fine and Performing Arts programs. The Arts faculty members play pivotal roles as conductors, directors, and curators. Students from across campus are drawn into the Arts activities, as participants or audience members, adding an often rich, occasionally controversial dimension to campus life. The theatres, galleries and music halls stand in stark contrast to the utilitarian and culturally banal character of most of the rest of the campus. The vitality, creativity, and often outrageous behaviour of creative Arts students adds a richness and depth to the undergraduate experience that is often underrated.

Some of the creative Arts disciplines are, perhaps surprisingly, finding a niche in the marketplace. Graduates in traditional Arts disciplines—drawing, painting, sculpture, classical music, and drama—continue to struggle to find career opportunities, but the more innovative areas in the Arts are doing better. The intersections of art and technology, art and engineering, and design generally are increasingly appreciated by employers. The shift in the digital economy from toolmakers (the technology) to tool users (the content) will likely attract greater attention in the years to come. There are some impressive Arts and technology collaborations across the country, demonstrating that the Arts can be connected to the emerging applied science–based economy.

Indeed, there are several excellent examples of how creative approaches to Arts education can generate excitement in the business community. Three digital media initiatives demonstrate the range and variety of initiatives. The Great Northern Way in Vancouver, a collaboration of Simon Fraser University, the University of British Columbia, the British Columbia Institute of Technology, and the Emily Carr University of Art + Design), has attracted considerable interest in the digital media industry. Similarly, the University of Waterloo–Stratford campus offers undergraduate and graduate degrees in digital media and, in its early operations, attracted very substantial student interest. (Conflict of interest notice: one of us was involved in the establishment of the campus.) The largest initiative is emerging out of the oddly named Ontario College of Art and Design University, a Toronto-based school that is an international leader in the commercialization of digital art and design. The impressive track record of Sheridan College in Ontario, one of the best animation schools anywhere, should have generated more imitators earlier, but the universities are coming around.

There is a final, completely overlooked, aspect of the fine Arts programs that warrants attention. Arts students are held to a high standard in terms of excellence, and they exercise this commitment to achievement very publicly. While most students work alone, producing essays, reports, and examinations that are rarely seen by anyone other than a faculty member, Arts students dance, sing, display, or otherwise show their work in public. From the outset, they know that their activities will be subject to the scrutiny and evaluation of their peers, a number of faculty members, and, often, the student body and members of the general public. Few other undergraduates wait anxiously for a newspaper review of their performance or presentation. Such a result is commonplace in the Arts.

Canadian universities need the Arts; indeed, it would be a good thing if more students were compelled to study in the field. A History of Fine Arts course, properly done, is one of the best possible introductions to the evolution of human civilization. Campuses would be much poorer places if robust and active Fine Arts departments, faculty, and students were not part of the university experience. But—and we must end with a resounding "but" in the interests of full disclosure, Fine and Performing Arts programs do not provide ready access to the workforce. If this is a priority, you would be well-advised to look to Fine and Performing Arts as a second major or a minor field and to capitalize on the rich extracurricular activities that these fields bring to the campus.

The "Man" Problem at Our Universities

Universities used to belong to men. In 1959 there were 3.25 men for every female undergraduate, and 5.5 men for every female graduate student, in Canada. The smaller number of women who attended universities clustered in "traditional" programs like nursing, English literature, languages, and home economics. Elementary school teachers, most of them women, did not need a degree before the 1960s. There were enough women around— searching (in the sexist vernacular of the time) for their "Mrs. Degree"—to ensure that campus life was sociable and civilized. But the universities were male. In 1971, 60 per cent of all university degrees were awarded to men, and virtually all the engineering, math, law, business, medicine, and science degrees went to them.

How much and how fast the tables have turned. By 2006, 63 per cent of Canadian university degrees went to women. In the same year, 57 per cent of all undergraduates enrolled full time (61 per cent part time) were women, which suggests they have a higher completion rate than men. The numbers seem to have levelled off. The balance is not shifting any further towards women (in 2008 they earned 60 per cent of degrees)—but men are not yet making a comeback within the academy. In 2008–2009, of the 1.12 million university students in Canada (full- and part-time), 471,000 were men and 640,000 were women. The 2010 *Maclean's* report on Canadian universities noted that at twenty-four of them, at least 60 per cent of the students were female.

At most Canadian medical schools, more women than men are studying to be doctors. Veterinarian medicine and pharmacy programs are attracting more women than men, and law schools—once the last preserve of the alpha male—are seeing more and more young women. Women still dominate fields like nursing, education, the humanities, and languages. But men do still hold a firm grip on the hard sciences, including mathematics, computer science, and engineering.

The academic success of young women is showing up across most of the university system. This is particularly true of Caucasian women, for males of Asian background are considerably keener about university than young men from traditional English and French backgrounds. It's not quotas or special arrangements that have allowed women to equal and even surpass men in many academic and professional areas. The women do well in hotly contested areas mostly because they study and work harder than men do. Or perhaps, as some have suggested, their brains are better wired for book learning.

Women are more likely to graduate from high school than men. They are more likely to go to university. They are more likely to graduate. They are at least as likely and, in a growing number of cases, more likely to get into the elite professional schools. Look at the lists of scholarship winners at high school and university graduations. There are lots of talented and hard-working men on the list, but in many instances the number of women outstrips their percentage of the school population.

Now, this would not be a big problem if it turns out that men have simply found a different path to training, career success, and happiness. Maybe, as some have suggested, men simply figured out earlier than women that there is a declining return on investment for university education. If so, they should dominate the colleges and trade schools. But they don't, for much the same pattern of "women rising" can be seen in college programs, apprenticeships, and even the paid workforce. The young men are not at university, nor are they showing up at other educational and training programs.

In the past, even this would not have been a crisis. Fifty years ago, male high school graduates or dropouts could find a good job in the factory, the lumber camp, with a trucking company, or in the oil patch. But most of these opportunities are gone, victims of outsourcing, global competition, the failure of Canadian competitiveness or, most of all, technological innovation. In the twenty-first century, low-skilled jobs for men means working in the service sector, where they find themselves competing for work with university graduates.

Now you can see the real problem. Men are not going to university in the expected numbers. They are not graduating with great career prospects. And the old default jobs—unskilled work—are declining in significance.

The potential impact of the new realities on patterns of partnerships, child-rearing, and the like could be considerable. Professions such as medicine and law will have to adapt to new gender realities. It appears that women practise medicine differently than men do. They spend more time, for example, with each patient and are less focused on producing income than their male counterparts are. Estimates indicate that it takes three female doctors to cover the clinical practices of two male doctors (although patient satisfaction is higher). The legal profession is struggling to balance its work- and billing-obsessed culture with respect for child-rearing and the desire of many female lawyers for a more sustainable work-life balance.

There's an added twist. It's long been common for professional men to marry less-educated women: the doctor marries the nurse, the executive the secretary, the lawyer the schoolteacher. It's less common for well-educated, accomplished women to marry less-educated men.

Perhaps Men Are Right

So, what happens to the young men who, in large and growing numbers, are not doing well in school, have trouble finding high-paying, stable jobs and a marriage partner, and don't seem to fit into the service-oriented twenty-first century economy?

We're in the midst of finding out. One segment of Canadian society—First Nations people—provides a grim warning. First Nations women are far more likely to go to university than men. Once educated, they tend to stay in urban centres and often marry outside their First Nation. The young men, in turn, are educationally disenfranchised, without work or prospects, and often live in communities where many of the most talented, well-educated, and active women have left. They often feel they have no future. The result? Frustration, anger, abuse, and self-destructive behaviour.

Elsewhere in Canadian society many families know exactly where these young men have gone. When you tell an audience that you have found the missing young men—they are in their parents' basements playing video games and working just enough to keep themselves in male toys—the bitter laughter from a sizable portion of the audience lets you know you are right. Add to this the reality of boomerang children—kids who return home after a period of near independence—and you have pinpointed one of the most serious generational challenges of the early twenty-first century.

Put some numbers to this trend and you realize that it's not a marginal statistical problem. The situation is already startling—at some institutions, the student body is close to 70 per cent female. Ontario estimates suggest that by the 2020s there will be 91,000 more women than men in the provincial university system. In short order there will be many more women in the professional workforce than men. The women are likely to find a receptive job market, for the collapse in the low-skill, high-wage "male" work of the 1960s and 1970s has been matched by the growth of opportunity in the social and health services, including nursing, geriatrics, and the like.

Many men need a university education, and universities require men. Yet very little is being done about this situation, nor in most places is it even discussed. We've hardly begun to look into why so few young men are in our classrooms. High schools have to figure out why males are tuning out and ignoring the challenges of scholarship and personal development. The change is so recent, so dramatic, and so unexpected that universities have not yet been able to respond.

Could it be that there is, in fact, no problem? That it's simply that men have decided that university degrees are not worth the effort required to earn them? Young men, so it is said, are more focused on career and income, they have listened closely to the growing chatter about the poor career options of university graduates—the jokes about English graduates asking, "Will you have fries with that?" Maybe women are deluding themselves, while the young men know more than the system does, and realize that a university degree is not a ticket to success. If so, maybe the absence of men simply means they have made wiser choices about their education than women have. But clearly the imbalance in the professional programs, at least, is worrying.

If the problem exists, what is to be done? First, universities and governments have to acknowledge the issue. Second, we need to know a lot more about the background and reasons for the dramatic shift. Third, university recruiting needs to be adjusted to speak directly to the young men, and it must address their reasons for avoiding the academy. Universities need to collaborate with colleges and employers to determine what is needed to attract young men to post-secondary and career-training opportunities. Fourth, parents need to be brought into the equation. They need to be mobilized to work with high school teachers and counsellors to ensure that young men understand the problems that await them if they do not prepare themselves properly for a career.

Finally, universities need to determine if their program mix, teaching style, or lack of perceived relevance is keeping young men away and—if the system is partially or substantially at fault—must adjust their operations to attract, retain, and graduate more young men.

Students Aren't Interested in Book Learning

Universities tell themselves many things to get them through the night. One of them is that most of their students are interested in the material they are studying. You don't have to spend much time in a classroom, or around students, to realize that this is partly a fantasy. Many students—just how many is difficult to determine, but it's probably a majority—have no deep interest in the material presented in class, or in what they read while preparing essays. They are willing to listen and be entertained, but they are not deeply engaged. To put it bluntly, they are not interested in book learning.

By book learning we mean the printed word, the storehouse of knowledge that has accumulated in books in the thousands of years since writing was invented, later in journals and newspapers, and now in electronic form. All disciplines are based on it: some—like history, English, and philosophy—almost totally. If you are going to get the most out of the study of political science, for example, you have to read—and read extensively. Students who come out of university knowing only what they have been told in class (assuming they know even that), and what they have researched for their written assignments, have learned only a fraction of what they should know. If they don't read on their own during—and especially after—their college days, they have to a large extent wasted their time.

It's not that no one reads books. Despite the Internet, book sales in Canada are reasonably healthy, or at least they are when the economy is good. Books are being bought and read, but students are not reading books that tell them about their country, the world, current events, past events, science, art, architecture, and politics—in other words, serious non-fiction. The same is true of serious fiction too: it would be interesting to find out how many students in English classes read novels (Michael Ondaatje, not J.K. Rowling) and poetry other than the assigned readings.

The habit of reading is best acquired early, and if young men and women arrive at university in their late teens having never read a serious book other than those a high school teacher forced them to read, they will probably never acquire it, especially if they don't pick it up during the course of their studies.

Students do not even turn to other sources for serious information. Ask a class how many read a newspaper regularly, and see if any hands go up. Usually there is silence, and the same is true of magazines—even *Maclean's*. Nor do they watch news on TV (though they're not missing much). The problem is particularly acute in the humanities and social sciences, which rely on book learning more than the natural and physical sciences do.

Ask students this question: Have you ever gone to the library to get a quotation or fact from a book for a term paper, started to leaf through the book, and become so interested you couldn't put it down? Very few will say yes, though of course the Internet has made it possible to write term papers without ever going to the library—or for that matter, ever getting out of bed.

There's nothing intrinsically wrong with a lack of interest in book learning. Not everything is for everybody. Some 15 per cent of Canadians have no interest in hockey (yes, it's true), but they don't spend their own and taxpayers' money attending hockey camps. The non-bookish, however, clog the universities. What do they retain from their studies? Most who graduate are more literate than when they went in—no mean accomplishment these days—but they retain little else, and have read as little as possible. Is this why we spend billions on post-secondary education?

Universities have a term these days for the habit of reading: they call it "life-long learning," and it's one of the things they are supposed to instill in their students. Clearly, with a great many students this is not being done, though it's not clear how the universities are supposed to do it. You can lead a horse to the river, but you can't make him drink, especially if he has no taste for water.

 # Campus Idealism Is Dead and Buried

Remember the youth culture of the 1960s and early 1970s? Students and faculty protested against the war in Vietnam, fought against racial discrimination, had as much sex and drugs as possible, supported full rights for gays and visible minorities, and battled against university administrations they thought were too chummy with the military, business, or the social status quo.

These were heady times for young people. There were sit-ins, teach-ins, be-ins, protests, and office occupations. Some were violent and destructive too, notably at Sir George Williams (now Concordia) University in January 1969. Radical music, Allen Ginsberg's poetry, Tom Robbins's books, and Timothy Leary's drug propaganda rocked university campuses. Then as now the American influence was strong. Students brought their anger and idealism into the classroom where, particularly among the younger professors, they found kindred spirits. Although they were always a minority—most students just wanted to get on with their studies—they made the campuses rock with energy and idealism.

Not any more. Save for some battles over Israeli issues, Canadian universities are pretty staid places. Forget the days when fiery speakers packed lecture halls with passionate students. Now it is Justin Trudeau, an establishment figure if there ever was one, who packs them in. Get Bill Gates or Jim Balsillie on campus and students will turn out in droves. Not too far right, though: the extremely conservative and abrasive Ann Coulter was too much for Carleton University to swallow.

The university teachers who got jobs in the 1960s and the 1970s were schooled in the language of revolution and protests. They weren't all hard-lefties by any means, but most were fairly liberal, and some carried a torch throughout their careers for the days when idealism dominated campus life. Those who are still teaching, and the younger colleagues who agree with their views, still struggle to stir up passions—against the war in Afghanistan, mistreatment of First Nations, social conservatism, America, or global warming—but nowadays, except at one or two campuses, without much success.

It's important to remember that the battles of the 1960s were mostly victories. Sexual freedom, anti-discrimination and human rights legislation, support for women, new approaches to First Nations affairs, a less-aggressive approach to overseas war, and so on are the direct result of '60s protests. And universities played a crucial role in the success of one of the most comprehensive social revolutions in history—the women's movement.

Where does that leave universities now? The standard view is that universities are leaders of social change, but this isn't really true. There are faculty and students who tilt against the windmills of the status quo, but they are a minority. Universities are on the whole mainstream institutions, supported by and reflecting the values of the dominant society. As such, they do more to illustrate broad values and assumptions than to challenge them.

We do not live in a radical age, particularly in Canada. Canada is a moderate country, proud of being nice, of avoiding conflict, and of focusing on stability and equality of opportunity. There are pockets of idealism—Native studies programs are a good example, although they have taken a practical turn of late—but our universities are career-building institutions, not cauldrons of radicalism and idealism.

Even in the 1960s Canadian universities were pretty tame places by global standards. Amidst the turmoil most students sought degrees, jobs, and a spot in the middle class. Now, universities are even more mainstream. Faculty care more about career advancement than pushing radical change. Students are preoccupied with practical objectives. Student unions are more likely to work with, rather than against, university administrations.

If idealism is weak or dying, it says more about Canadian society as a whole than it does about the universities. Students should be worried about global warming, but that strikes too close to their quality of life—when we meet the enemy, only to find it's us, it's hard to work ourselves into a righteous frenzy. The calmness and practicality of the university system reflects the high level of comfort most Canadians have with their lives. We don't live in a radical time. We are not seeking major societal change. We have no grand issues. And so universities, reflecting the society in which they exist, have become quiet, even complacent places.

Part-time Student Work and the Beer Index

From time to time we've conducted little experiments in which we ask our classes, by a show of hands, a couple of questions. First, how many work for wages during the academic year, and second, how many work more than ten hours a week. The results are always the same: roughly two-thirds, sometimes more, answer yes to the first, and a quarter or so say yes to the second. Some work twenty hours a week or more while taking a full course load.

This does not include student-parents who, whether they also work for wages or not, must have no spare time at all. We are talking here about students in the traditional age group who attend class fifteen hours a week, do lab work, write essays, study for tests, and also work in bars, restaurants, or similar places.

Why do they do this? For many, it's the desire to avoid graduating with a large student debt. You can hardly blame a student for not wanting to start life owing $25,000 or more. The cost of tuition, room and board, books, and pocket money can be $15,000 a year, and it's tough to find a summer job that will pay that much in four or five months, though some students manage to do so. For others, it's a lifestyle choice: a car, an iPod, or computer games.

What these students miss, however, is one of the greatest gifts that a university can give—leisure time. For undergraduates who do not need to work for wages, even for those in demanding science programs with heavy lab work, there will be many free hours in the week. They can socialize, debate, hang out, join clubs and political societies, sing in the choir, conduct lab experiments on their own, and most of all, they can haunt the library and read. Self-education is a huge part of the university experience. Students who learn only what they hear in class have lost a big chunk of what they should have gained from university, and this is a tremendous pity.

In a way, though, you can hardly blame them. The cost of the lighter side of university life is much greater than it was two generations ago. In the mid 1960s, you could buy a ten-ounce glass of beer in Ontario for fifteen cents, and the minimum wage was $1.50 an hour. That's ten glasses of beer for an hour's work. Now a similar amount of (imported) suds costs about $3, with a minimum wage of about $9 an hour. That's three glasses of beer for an hour's work, disregarding taxes, which are also much higher now. So the "Beer Index," a rough-and-ready guide to the cost of student living, has more than tripled. Forty years ago it was not necessary to make a choice between beer and other expenses. Now it is. No wonder students find they have to work.

Students Are No Longer in Awe of Their Professors

And perhaps this isn't a bad thing. Years ago, university teachers had the image of being highly intelligent but a bit weird: the classic "absent-minded professor." You wouldn't ask them for directions, or how to fix your car, but they certainly knew a lot.

Many graduates from the years before the 1990s remember fondly the erudition, wisdom, and insight of some of their professors. They quoted the Bible or Marx at will, called on a vast storehouse of information, and seemed to have a bibliographic file box fixed to their brains. Students were in awe, amazed that they had so much knowledge at their fingertips. The eighteenth-century poet Oliver Goldsmith said it best:

> *And still they gazed, and still the wonder grew*
> *That one small head could carry all he knew.*

Times have changed. Faculty still know tons of stuff, and most can fill you with as much information as you can hold. The most popular professors are often charismatic lecturers—may it always be thus—or great teachers, but the mystique is largely gone. Students often address their professors by their first names and have clearly taken them down from their pedestals.

The belief in faculty expertise, and in expertise more generally, has been undercut by three elements. First, high school students are encouraged to have and to hold strong opinions, rewarded as much for speaking their minds as for having something to say. Praised for making an effort— "Good job, Susie!"—rather than being right, they are impatient with being corrected.

Second, people born after 1970, those who began to come to university in the 1990s, were not trained to respect their "elders" and other authority figures in the way their parents were. "Never trust anyone over thirty" has had a profound effect on relations between the generations.

The Internet is the other expertise killer. *Wikipedia*—which many in the university love to hate, but which is actually both useful and mostly accurate—along with Google and the like, are but a few of the Internet tools available to anyone anywhere, including in the middle of classes. Professors can still be knowledgeable and impressive, but the average undergraduate can find a great deal of information—and many answers—with a few keystrokes. It's a whole different ball game in class when instructors find students fact-checking their lectures on laptops.

Specialization is also changing the very nature of academic expertise. Once trained as generalists, with a broad grounding in a discipline, faculty are more and more narrowly focused. Why? Because knowledge is expanding so fast that it's hard to keep up in the broader discipline.

And so the awe is largely gone from the university experience. Faculty are still just as smart, but the classic man or woman of letters—erudite and deeply informed—is increasingly rare. Students are blasé in the extreme. Profs know stuff. They are aggregators of knowledge, facilitators of learning, and mentors extraordinaire. But they are rarely seen as fonts of wisdom and repositories of the knowledge of the ages.

The Entitlement Generation Has Changed the Game

A decade ago faculty members at a Maritime university started complaining over coffee about their students' behaviour in class: inconsistent attendance, lack of respect for professors, poor classroom behaviour, litigiousness, and a reluctance to complete assignments. At a meeting with high school counsellors, they asked an obvious question: "what is going on with the current group of students?" The reply was unexpected: "If you think this is bad, wait until you see the Grade 9s that are coming." It's true. Something new and nasty is going on with university students these days, and there's more trouble in store.

Every generation claims that the next one has been coddled and spoiled, but it really may be true this time. There are dozens of explanations for the remarkable freedom, high expectations, and unreasonable demands of today's youth. There's the guilt and the money of two-income families, societal permissiveness, child-centred educational and parenting styles, overwhelming materialism, video games, sexualized media, and on and on.

The changes in the student psyche are not all bad, of course. These "spoiled" students are more assertive, very confident, able and willing to express their opinions, not intimidated by adults and professors, and very sure of themselves.

But they also have a deep sense of entitlement. They expect material well-being and an easy passage through school, university, and work. They expect a great deal from their professors and university staff and can be quite nasty if those expectations are not met. Their evaluations of their profs can be devastating.

They often expect deadlines to be altered, want their explanations accepted without confirmation, and try to insist that course requirements fit their availability to do work. Not all students fit this description, but the general student population has changed.

The entitlement generation had it pretty good at home and in school, and they expect this to continue at university and in the workforce. They are used to parents and other adults responding to their demands and have developed a pretty limitless sense of their future prospects. When these students reach university they bring a lifetime of being celebrated at every turn and of being protected from the realities of life and hardship.

The entitlement students are causing quite a problem on campus, not least by reducing the attractiveness of the classroom and the joy of teaching. The complaining of the most-demanding minority really upsets faculty members, who expect deference—if not respect and awe—from their students.

The university system has adapted in dramatic ways. Check out the food in the cafeteria, the additional facilities in the residences, the greater flexibility of many faculty members, and the declining work demands on the students. These young people, however over-entitled they may be, are the universities' clients, after all, and they have to be kept content, if not completely happy. Universities continue to adapt to the students, perhaps not realizing that responding to the demands for change will fuel even higher expectations.

The entitlement generation seems to be gradually importing the assumptions and demeanour of parenting and the school system into post-secondary education. There is a grave inconsistency between the requirements for academic excellence and professional achievement and the student-pleasing priorities of the youth-centred realities of our time. It remains to be seen what gives first: the standards and requirements of the academy or the expectations and demands of young people.

In other chapters we question whether universities will continue to shape themselves according to student wishes, or whether they will retreat to a more traditional curriculum. History suggests a bet on the university is safe, but a visit to a high school leaves the impression that it's a risky gamble. Youth may well win out—at considerable cost to the universities, the future work force, and the country.

51 Eighteen Is the New Fifteen

We love our students. Honest. If we were writing this in the late 1960s and early 1970s, we might well be complaining about the students' long hair, contempt for authority, and preference for narcotic substances. But times change, and this generation—like all generations—has certain defining characteristics that need to be acknowledged and understood. Students need to know that we have them sussed out a little. Parents need to know that we understand their children. And faculty and staff at university need to see in writing what they live with on a daily basis. What follows has not been researched and is a vast generalization. But it's what we (the authors) think and what we experience.

There's no polite way of saying this: many of today's students, particularly the young men, are not very mature. "Big shock!" scream parents across the country. It's well known that young people today—and oh, it makes us feel old to write that—are not as self-reliant and independent as in the past. The reasons for this are many: a child-centred and limited-discipline education system, spoiling by parents, the "everyone's a winner" ethos that has eliminated failure from the lives of many (particularly the well-to-do), and the high level of creature comforts enjoyed by many in Canadian society.

Whatever the reasons, the outcome is remarkable. University students act younger than ever. Their birth certificates say they are eighteen, but their behaviour and attitude suggest that they are fifteen. They do not show the maturity of their years—and expectations for eighteen-year-olds have not always been particularly high—and some serious problems are emerging. Some young men seem to make particularly bad choices and find themselves in serious difficulties. They do not manage their time well, shirk their responsibilities, and have a problem exercising their freedom. If you do not believe us, ask eighteen-year-old girls, who are often quick to comment on the shortcomings of their classmates on the maturity scale.

We leave this with you to ponder, for the observation is so impressionistic that elaboration would be misleading. First-year students, the classic eighteen-year-olds, are being asked to make huge decisions of great importance to their long-term development. Universities and society at large insist on a high level of independence—young people this age can drive, vote, and join the army—but leave them with little armour at one of the most challenging points in their lives. Academic systems assume and even demand a high level of maturity. If our impression is right—and we are confident that it is—then there's a major disconnect between the world of young adults, particularly the men, and the expectations and processes of the university system.

A Different Philosophy of Education

Several times in this book we have suggested that students graduating from high school these days have been sheltered from the reality of what awaits them in university and after. The startling statistic quoted earlier that about three-quarters of first year university students get lower grades than in high school, some much lower, a quarter do the same, and fewer than 3 per cent do better, shows the disconnect between high school and university standards.

High schools weren't always like this in Canada, though, and here we enter a world that may seem unbelievable, though it was real enough to anyone now over 65. Most Canadian high school students lived in this world, but we will take Ontario as an example. Fifty years ago, in that province, the high schools were "streamed," and by their second year students were in the collegiate, the commercial, or the technical program, all of which had different classes. Commercial and technical students graduated at the end of Grade XII (for some reason they used Roman numerals then), but the collegiate students, the ones headed for university, took an extra year, the legendary Grade XIII.

What made Grade XIII notorious were the examinations that took place at the end of the year, on which university entrance was based. These were popularly called the "provincials," because every student in the province wrote the same exam at the same time, and the papers were graded, anonymously, in Toronto. Most amazing of all, the entire year's grade was based on the exam result. Let us repeat that: the school had no input at all into the year's grade; 100 per cent of the result was based on a single exam. Students needed to pass nine of these exams to get into university. Languages had two exams—English literature, English composition, French literature, French composition, and so on, and one for each of the maths and sciences. The results came out in August, and were published in the local newspapers. You looked up your name and the number beside it. If it said "Smith 9," you were off to university; if it said "Smith 8" or less, you were back for another year of high school (and in those days no one called it a "victory lap"; it was a mark of shame).

Students nowadays, for whom Grade 12 is often one long celebration of their supposed achievements, and whose acceptance at university often comes in the spring of Grade 12, based on the final marks in Grade 11, might well imagine how stressful this old system was. Nine exams over a two-week period, with the results made public only a few weeks before you hoped to be going to university. Students obsessed about them, lost sleep, hired tutors. Imagine also the pressure it put on high schools and individual teachers, for whom the system was a kind of assessment: Did school A have a better graduation rate than school B? Did the students of algebra teacher A have a better pass rate than the students of algebra teacher B? Of course they did, and this led to stress as well.

This system had a long history in Ontario. Students studying geometry in the spring of 1959 bought a booklet containing the questions from all the geometry exams for the previous thirty years, from 1928 to 1958. The questions of course were not identical, but the course material was exactly the same. Students answered the questions in those exams as preparation for their own ordeal. If you could do them, your forthcoming exam lost its terror.

The great advantage to this system was its uniformity. It didn't matter what school you were at; if you got 75 per cent in trigonometry at an upper-middle class school in Toronto, you were no better and no worse than a student who got the same grade in Fort Frances. The universities could rely on the grades as a kind of Canadian version of the American SAT. A decent grade in English meant that you could write, and would have no trouble in a social sciences or humanities major at university. For many students, university was easier than high school, because they no longer had to take maths or sciences beyond the obligatory first year science course for Arts students.

In the 1960s, opposition to the system mounted. Teachers and schools whose students did worse than the provincial average had never liked it, and it ran counter to the student-centered climate of that decade, fostered particularly by the Ontario Institute for Studies in Education, which had very liberal views on the subject. The main criticism was that the old system had "taught the subject rather than the student," and it was true that, in teaching algebra, the feelings of individual students about algebra were rarely taken into consideration. In the mid-sixties the system was changed so that results from the schools made up 50 per cent of the final grade and, at the end of the decade, it was abolished altogether so that the schools began providing 100 per cent of the grade. Almost immediately, grade inflation began: while the average grade of a student entering UBC, to pick an example from another province, was 70 per cent in 1970, it is now close to 90 per cent.

Was it a bad system? The answer depends on your view of education. It was certainly stressful, and the opposite of student-friendly. It made it difficult for late bloomers to get into university (adult students had to go to night school, then write the same exams). The "streaming" system also separated the university-bound kids from the others by the age of fifteen, something that is no longer done—at least not as openly. It did, however, mean that those who survived it could be sure that they had the tools to be successful in university. No one standing at the front of a university class had cause to complain (though sometimes they did) that their students couldn't write a coherent sentence. It was also a reliable standard for university admissions officers, something that we badly lack today. It's all theoretical anyway: given the public's desire to see their children at university, the strength of educational theorists, and the power of teachers' unions, it's inconceivable that such a system could ever be reintroduced in this country.

We Should Demand More, Not Less, from Our Students

A few years back a university was developing a marketing plan aimed at incoming students. "It's All About You!!!" the promotional material sang— sending precisely the wrong message. University is not all about students, or shouldn't be. The current pattern of seeing students as customers, to be cultivated and pampered, is fundamentally wrong.

Universities have stopped expecting an all-out effort from students. While failure is still a possibility at university, in many programs passing does not require the same effort it did a few decades ago. Much of the responsibility for success has shifted from the student to the institution. Universities now offer all measure of remedial assistance, disability supports, accommodations, and exemptions. Professors often shy away from high-level demands because they generate student anger, lengthy student appeals, and all manner of other challenges. Did any Canadian university have a "Student Success Centre" in 1960? If so we haven't heard of it. In 1960, student success was up to the student.

This doesn't happen in other areas of high-level performance. Coaches don't exempt players from practice because they are having a hard day. They don't mollycoddle and cajole, nor do they entice and gently encourage. They bellow and demand. They exist as a presence in athletes' minds even when they are not around. No one tries to make sure the athletes had a good time and felt comfortable with their effort. The goal is winning; the requirement full-out effort. It's the same in the performing arts. Top ballet and music teachers press and insist. Top-level sports and high-quality music and dance require total effort and commitment—from both those in training and those training them.

Why don't we see such commitment in other disciplines? To stick to the sports analogy, university has shifted from being an elite athletic competition to being an intramural event. It's like giving the participants in water polo—an intense and brutal sport, requiring great strength, speed, and stamina—inner tubes to help them float. It's fun, easy to learn, doesn't require maximum effort and allows everyone to play—but it doesn't produce champions. Instead, it produces graduates who have been encouraged, celebrated for small successes, and permitted to operate in a world of false competition and minimal achievement.

Champions do exist in small numbers in Canada but in much higher numbers in China, Korea, Japan, and India. The top graduates of these countries—and elite American schools—have the attitudes and abilities that push their nation forward. Canadian graduates too often feel better about themselves and their accomplishments than they should. A cruel, competitive world, one that rewards hard-driving winners and casts aside those with a sense of entitlement, awaits.

 # In Praise of Single Parents

Many students work hard, but there's a special category we'd like to mention: single parents, almost all of them women, who attend classes, care for their children, and sometimes work part or full time.

We stand in awe of a student who can get up in the morning, take her kids to school or daycare, come to campus, attend lectures, take notes, work on term papers, study, come home, pick up the kids, cook dinner, leave the kids with a grandparent or other baby-sitter, work a shift somewhere, come back and study, then get up the next morning and do it all over again. If the student can't manage a full five-course load, she will either take summer courses, or if she works full time in the summer, her undergraduate career will be six years or more instead of four.

We even knew (and we hope our surprise is not sexist), a man who did this—a young fellow left with a two-year-old daughter. He attended classes full time, earned good grades, worked long shifts as a bouncer in a bar, found care for his daughter, and is now a successful lawyer. Good for him.

The motivation of these students is obvious—a desire to care for their children and to provide a better life for themselves and their families—and most of them show tremendous dedication to their studies. Few, in fact, ask for special privileges or even draw attention to their family circumstances. They are not looking for sympathy or academic concessions, even though most faculty make accommodations when family circumstances warrant.

Some of these student/parents live close to grandparents who can look after the children during school hours. Others find subsidized spots in university daycare centres, though these have lengthy waiting lists. Still others share the responsibilities with other students, usually through elaborate timetable negotiations. In a real pinch some parents bring babies and toddlers to campus, worried about disrupting the lectures but desperate not to miss classes.

Many single parents have little money. Student loans and, if they are lucky, access to family housing on campus, help pay the bills—all the while adding to debt. Many of these students, of course, have to find part-time jobs to supplement their incomes, adding to child-care challenges, detracting from homework time, and compounding the difficulties of attending school. Canada's financial aid requirements have provisions for single parents and their children, but some of this will eventually have to be paid back. While most Canadians are comfortable with the idea of a young adult's making do on a heavy overdose of macaroni and cheese, many would be concerned about the single parent student's ability to feed, clothe, and otherwise support her children this way.

Single parents often stand out. They are typically among the most dedicated in class, and they have little time for young adult slackers who do not take advantage of their educational opportunities. They are highly motivated, if only because of the personal and financial sacrifice that they and their children are making. The single parents are often perennially tired, exhausted by the constant balancing act, and the pressures of combining parenting and academic studies.

So, save a special cheer at convocation for the single parents crossing the stage. They are often identified by the loud "Way to go, Mom!" yell that comes from the audience. Rest assured that the faculty members on the stage, aware of the challenges of the single moms and dads, are cheering too. As for us, we'd like to give them a medal.

Eighteen-Year-Olds Control Our Universities

More than thirty years ago, at a university we won't name—oh, what the hell, it was UBC—several physical education students gathered in a student advising area at the beginning of term. They had to declare a major and, since many aspired to be schoolteachers, they were searching for a second "teachable" subject. Three of them, after deep thought, settled on geography. Their rationale? The building where the geography courses were taught was several blocks closer to the gym than the buildings where history and English students studied.

Such shallowness is, we hope, not universal, but the situation exposes a weakness of the Canadian university system. It's clear that Canadian universities are very student-centric, trying to attract and retain as many students as possible. It's also clear that our universities, like Canadian society as a whole, are driven by personal choice more than by the needs of society. The idea of acting in the best interests of the province or the country takes a distant back seat to the desire to do what the individual wants to do.

People rarely discuss the implications of these realities. But consider this. Over time, universities respond to student demand. If the students start to bunch up in one or two areas—like psychology in the 1970s, computer science in the 1990s, accounting and business in the past twenty years— there is great pressure to expand course and program offerings. Faculty members in the high-demand fields clamour for more resources, citing unprecedented enrolment figures to back up their requests. Eventually, the number of faculty positions, staff members, and classrooms adjusts to student numbers.

Result: the collective decisions of tens of thousands of eighteen-year-olds—and of these students as they work their way through their degrees— determine the shape of the Canadian university system and the expenditure of billions of dollars.

This is fine when the marketplace aligns, in its mysterious way, with the academic interests of university students. In the 1960s and 1970s things aligned, largely because university-educated students were in short supply and jobs were abundant. By the 1980s, the supply and demand curves had separated, particularly at the level of individual programs. So, at times, Canadian universities produced too many schoolteachers, or not enough. The same is true of medical doctors and nurses. Currently the Canadian economy is short of engineers, medical professionals, and other highly technical graduates, while the number of humanities and social science grads is not well matched with career opportunities.

Universities do make choices, largely by regulating entry—there are only so many seats in the classrooms, after all—although even that has proven remarkably elastic in recent years. This, in turn, makes these programs more competitive, allowing departments and faculties to select just the students they want. The other, more open-entry areas end up with a broader cross-section of the incoming population. It's harder to get into engineering than mathematics—programs requiring much the same level of ability and skill—and much easier to get into first-year arts than law school. Interestingly, education programs are among the most difficult to get into across the country, largely because they provide a straight-line route to a comfortable middle-class career.

Of course, when governments have tried to regulate the production of graduates in specified fields they have been sharply criticized and, more often than not, have judged demand incorrectly. Part of the current shortage of medical doctors was created by decisions to hold back the growth of medical schools over the past two decades.

Universities find it very difficult to shift resources because of the long-term commitment to full-time faculty positions. As they struggle with an ossified version of supply meeting demand, they are essentially aligning themselves with the interests and preferences of young Canadians. This is an acceptable choice if everyone understands that's what's happening and if we all agree young adults are best able to determine how the country should spend its money.

It's a much less acceptable choice if governments, the general public, and employers expect something different. When there's a general belief that universities exist to serve the broader interests of society, as well as the personal academic and career interests of students, the current practice runs off the rails. A few countries direct students towards specific fields and engage in social engineering to produce the "right" number of graduates in the "right" fields. Canada is far removed from this approach and seems content with leaving the shape of the nation's universities largely in the hands of eighteen-year-olds.

Aboriginal Students Put Their Communities First

The change in Aboriginal participation in the Canadian university system has been extraordinary. In the late 1960s only a couple of hundred Aboriginal students attended university. There are now more than 30,000 Aboriginal students in Canada's colleges and universities. And—common assumptions aside—they do not all receive massive subsidies and grants to attend university, even though the Government of Canada has made commitments to expanding financial support for them.

There are some important trends associated with Aboriginal participation. The overwhelming majority of Aboriginal students are female—as much as 85 per cent in some regions—and many of them are single parents. Success rates are not very high, largely because of the gap between the academic standards of predominantly Aboriginal schools and the urban upper-middle-class schools that produce most university students.

Aboriginal students tend to cluster in programs with special support programs, particularly in education and social work, but with expanding numbers in law, administration, nursing, and business. Few special efforts are made to produce Aboriginal historians, biologists, or philosophers, although there are increasing numbers of all of these. The Aboriginal graduates are impressive, determined, and dedicated students, often overcoming enormous personal, family, and community challenges to complete their education.

But by far the greatest difference between Aboriginal and non-Aboriginal students is that Aboriginal people put their communities ahead of their own ambition and opportunity. There is a remarkably common question that Aboriginal students ask, in one form or another, of professors, counsellors, and others: How can I best use my education to benefit my community? It's not a question you'll often hear from a non-Aboriginal student.

The reasons for, and the effect of, this desire to put the community first are quite simple. Young Aboriginal people know how badly their communities and organizations need trained and skilled people. Their parents, teachers, community members, and—particularly—elders often push talented young people hard to succeed at school and go on to university. What's more, Aboriginal people often place a much higher value on community than the highly individualistic non-Aboriginal student population.

This is why Aboriginal students are more likely to pursue careers of direct benefit to their communities, often broadly defined, and why they are much more likely to see their talents and abilities as a collective resource. It also means that Aboriginal students carry the burdens of their family and community into their studies and often see failure not in personal terms, but rather as though they have let down their community.

There's a remarkable success story in the Aboriginal experience at university. There are now thousands of graduates across the country, moving into various private and public sector positions and enriching and empowering both their communities and the nation. There are now many Aboriginal professional associations—the country is long since past the point where an indigenous PhD, doctor, teacher, lawyer, nurse, or business owner was a rarity. The impact of Aboriginal teacher-education programs alone has had a tremendous impact on Aboriginal education in Canada. And there is now a higher percentage of Aboriginal people with law degrees than the percentage of lawyers for the whole population.

The situation is not all rosy, however. Many of the people who leave remote reserve communities to attend university do not go back. This is particularly true for Aboriginal women, who often remain in the cities and large towns and often marry a non-Aboriginal. Even so, the Aboriginal graduates see their accomplishments and their obligations in very different terms than other university students, who routinely place their careers and personal interests well in front of doing what's best for their community or their country.

Cheating and the Internet

Cheating is as old as education, and no doubt began when the first teacher tested the first student. Plato's students probably brought notes into his exams scratched on pieces of pottery. They might have hired an older student to sit their exams, or paid some poor scribe a few drachmas to write their essays. But the days of cheat notes on *ostraka* are long gone. Now students have discovered a whole new world of cheating, with the Internet.

The Internet has proved a powerful tool for illegal academic behaviour. It was bad enough when desktop computers began to provide access to vast amounts of information and "cutting and pasting" was transformed from a kindergarten activity into an essay-building process. Then intellectual criminals—no need to mince words here—created websites where students could buy and download entire essays. Some sites allowed students to specify the grade they wanted: an A, B, or C. No need to draw attention by having a C+ student submit an A+ paper. Writers can earn substantial incomes producing individually written papers for lazy and dishonest students.

Universities are smart places so they quickly found a response. A web service called turnitin.com found its niche in electronically surveying essays for universities to check for plagiarism. It compared this year's papers to ones from earlier years, and to essays handed in at other universities. Students, when caught, are given a small penalty, usually a failing grade on the course (but rarely a permanent mark on the transcript, thus removing a crucial piece of information for potential employers).

Their explanations are usually lame: too much academic work (university's fault), have to work to afford school (parents' fault), didn't know plagiarism was wrong (society's fault), need high grades to get into law school or medicine or to get professional accreditation in engineering or accountancy (the system's fault), paying high sums as an international student and struggling not to disappoint parents (globalization's fault), and on and on.

The problem now extends well beyond copying essays. With the newer technologies, particularly Internet-enabled mobile phones, students can bring the entire textbook—and a thousand other texts for that matter—into an exam setting. Universities can and do fight back. Mobile devices are banned from examination rooms. Signals can be jammed. But with the stakes high and the demand growing, student and criminal ingenuity will continue the process of innovation in academic dishonesty.

There is one good piece of news in all of this. There aren't many crooked students. The vast majority are honest and sincere. They do their homework properly, don't cheat on tests, and use assignments and examinations as learning opportunities. So far at least, the cheaters have not taken over the academy. But it's certainly demoralizing that even a small number have been caught.

What's more important is that cheating (especially when widespread in a particular class or program) undermines the very purpose of the academic enterprise. So far there have been no public scandals about academic integrity. Universities keep these cases quiet where they can. Some day soon, though, a big scandal may break out and, potentially, tarnish the public reputation of the academy.

There's good reason to anticipate that the problem will get worse. The Internet has also transformed thousands of young people—maybe most of them—into petty thieves. The young steal constantly. They rip off music and damage an entire industry. They download movies—most are available on-line the day they enter the theatres—and wreak havoc with the intellectual property of newspapers, publishers, composers, artists, and filmmakers. Check a young adult's iPod, BlackBerry, computer, or other device and you might well find hundreds of dollars worth of stolen content. Parents who would be devastated if their children stole a chocolate bar from the local convenience store think nothing of their kids' scouring the web for the latest film and downloading it onto their computers.

The Internet has damaged one of the core moral and commercial principles of our society: that creators own their intellectual property. Young people are remarkably casual about stealing and using what is not theirs. It's not a huge step from downloading movies without paying for them to grabbing an essay or other content off the web and submitting it as one's own. Given that very little is being done to prevent young people from committing this kind of intellectual crime, it is not hard to imagine that the Internet will continue to undermine intellectual integrity, promote dishonesty, and blur the line between original and borrowed ideas.

58 Students Are Unwilling to Study Abroad

Only 3 per cent of Canadian university students study abroad during their undergraduate years. That's amazing, given that Canadian institutions have dozens of exchange agreements with foreign universities. Our universities offer travel study courses. Queen's University even has a castle in England. Other universities have field stations and campuses in exotic locations. There are hundreds of scholarships and bursaries for international experiences and work placement overseas for adventurous students.

Universities want their students to travel and learn abroad. Professors know the many benefits that come from living overseas. Language and culture programs in particular want students to spend time in a linguistically rich educational environment. French students can go to France (or Quebec if they cannot afford overseas travel), German students to Germany, Asian studies students to Japan, China, or Korea.

There are dozens of signs on every campus promoting travel study classes, exchange agreements, and international bursaries. International offices host information nights and promote overseas experiences. Professors talk up opportunities in class. Many faculty members volunteer to lead students abroad. But few students want to go.

Why is it so? Students in Europe—helped by well-funded European Union exchange agreements—move about regularly. So do Aussies and Kiwis. But Canadians, exposed in schools and communities to people from around the world, just don't seem keen to travel. Maybe they think that visiting the Asian community of Richmond, BC, the Ukrainian-Canadians of Dauphin, Manitoba, or Little Italy in Toronto is a substitute for the real thing.

Money is a big factor. International travel can be expensive. Highly motivated students find the cash and make the sacrifices necessary to participate. And there are substantial and helpful bursaries available at most universities. Many of the exchange agreements have students pay their fees and room and board at their home universities. The incremental cost is limited to travel expenses (and enough money to pay for local experiences). Governments are getting on the bandwagon. Ontario, in particular, is keen to promote study abroad.

Language used to be a barrier. Unlike European young adults, who are comfortable in several languages, most Canadian students, like their American counterparts, want only English-language instruction. But many universities now offer English-language courses abroad, often taught by native English speakers and patterned on standard North American courses. It's not a genuine cultural experience, but it's a start, and it removes a major disincentive to overseas study.

The main resistance to studying abroad is cultural. Despite Canada's ethnic diversity, this is a parochial country. Young adults, in the main, are neither worldly nor adventurous. They stick close to home. Even students born and raised abroad appear to limit their travel to return visits to the home country. Canadian youth lack the wanderlust of Scandinavian, Australian, and New Zealand youth. Those who do study abroad tend to cluster by native tongue, limiting contact with local people. In terms of cultural learning, the best thing that can happen for a Canadian student is to get a local boyfriend or girlfriend.

In the globalized, internationally connected world, overseas experience has become a prerequisite for national success. The country needs young people who know Japan, Korea, China, India, the Middle East, Brazil, and other countries and areas well, who speak the language, and who understand local cultures and political environments. The ethnic diversity within Canada needs to be matched by solid connections to the rest of the world.

Universities have to lead this push and urge students to explore distant lands, learn new languages, experience other cultures, and become citizens of the world. To date, Canada and its universities are not doing very well.

Residence Life

A month before the University of Northern British Columbia opened in September 1994 the university learned that the furniture for the residences, including the beds, would not arrive on time. With students arriving in a few weeks, the university hastily made alternate arrangements with city hotels. About 400 brand-new students started their careers in temporary quarters, taking buses to and from the campus. When the beds (but not the tables and chairs) arrived, the university shut down the hotel option and the students camped out in their residence rooms. They were not happy, but eventually order was restored. Not an ideal situation, but one that bonded the first-year students and created one of UNBC's first folk memories.

Residences are not simply an "ancillary service" designed to assist students with housing needs. They are an integral part of the academic experience, crucial to student success, and fundamentally important to the nature and vitality of campus life.

First impressions count, and so do first-year experiences. Many students arrive at university full of nervous energy. Away from their parents, among strangers, in a new environment, they experience a combination of liberty and rules, control and freedom. Residences, largely through residence dons (advisors) and residence life programs, monitor the young people, control (most) excesses, and otherwise help students survive and thrive in a strange land.

Residences do more than any other part of the university to tie students to a campus. They provide shared experiences—social occasions, personal oversight, gentle direction—and common disgust with residence food has bound generations of students together. Countless friendships, hookups, and romances find their origins in residence cafeterias, dorms, games rooms, and events. Residences ease students from parental control into adulthood and they do so in an arms-length and often very dynamic fashion.

Many students never experience residence life and they are often the poorer for it. Those who commute to campus typically stay with their parents, remain connected to familiar friends and activities, and are pulled away from full engagement in the campus. For them, university attendance lingers for several years as an extension of high school. At the other extreme, students attending universities where most students live in residence—Acadia, Mount Allison, St. Francis Xavier, Bishop's—where the institution dwarfs and defines the host community, have intense experiences that shape their adulthood.

The more in-tune universities understand that residence life is interconnected with academic development. Living-learning communities knit them together nicely. Lectures, seminars, study sessions, and help centres in the residences enrich both the community and the students' academic experience.

Most Canadian universities lag well behind American schools in the development of residence life. Private schools in the states compete for students more with hot tubs and climbing walls than with faculty publications and remedial writing seminars. The elite private institutions offer residence-life arrangements that seem more like academic resorts than university housing. Food courts, however, demonstrate how much has changed. Largely gone are the lineups for the daily dose of mac and cheese or meat loaf, or as at Western in the 1960s, the "dreaded veal cutlet." In their place are multi-island, customer-driven food emporiums. Mom's cooking quickly recedes into memory, replaced by a culinary cornucopia, particularly if you share the food preferences of eighteen-year-old males. *Bon appétit!*

VI
A Professor's
Life

Too Much Research?

Every so often universities evaluate themselves, and usually come up with a "mission statement." Almost always they conclude that mission is to teach and to carry out research. Even the small ones say this; no Canadian university will state that its faculty members are not interested in research and that it is primarily a teaching university, though some colleges offering university courses will give this as an enticement to students. While teaching-first institutions are common in the USA, Canadian universities are firmly committed to the research-teaching scholar model. Faculty members are assigned, by convention, 40 per cent of their time to research, the same as for income-generating and student-serving teaching activities (the other 20 per cent goes to committee and administrative work).

The research scholar model that emerged from the expansion of the university system in the 1960s was embraced enthusiastically by faculty members and supported by government. In very real ways, scholarly research had profound impacts across society. Work being done by Canadian academics was contributing to and being influenced by a changing world. The range of those contributions was astounding: political research was at the forefront of the Cold War, the Green Revolution, and the rise of the consumer society; medical advances transformed public and private health care; and innovations in the social sciences and humanities transformed public attitudes to race, gender, sexuality, privilege, colonialism, and the like. The more that Canadians outside of the academy found themselves benefiting from it, the more readily were public investments in academic work justified.

While some of this scholarly output is important and even brilliant, the growing reality is that, in some fields, there is too much of it. The global expansion of the university system has unleashed a tsunami of academic research that, in most fields, is out of proportion to the ability of faculty members to keep abreast of latest developments. The proliferation of academic journals and books—even before the advent of the Internet cranked up the flood of new and recycled ideas to unimaginable levels, and before the East and South Asian universities came fully on stream—exceeded the capacity of specialists to stay on top of their fields. As a direct result, most scholars turned their attention to sub- or sub-sub-disciplines, working on narrower fields and speaking to ever-smaller audiences.

For fifty years and more, universities have promoted the idea that the best teachers are the ones most active in research, because they bring the "cutting edge" of their disciplines into the classroom. In many fields, however, particularly in the sciences, the gap between the frontiers of research and undergraduate study is so big that the translation from the laboratory to the classroom is all but impossible. Moreover, some very good researchers are dreadful teachers, or really don't like teaching. The truth is that students, especially at the beginning level, can be served extremely well by teaching-focused faculty members who may or may not do any research at all. Universities really need a balance of research-intensive and teaching-only faculty. Similarly, the Canadian system needs more teaching-centred universities and fewer that claim to be research-intensive.

There is also growing evidence that the proliferation of scholarship has gotten out of hand. How many books, articles, and dissertations have been written on Shakespeare? No one knows for sure, but the *World Shakespeare*

Bibliography Online lists 120,000 entries. Is there need, or room, for more? Studies have shown that, faced with an ever-growing mountain of scholarship, faculty members are actually reading less, because of the system-wide emphasis on producing scholarship, rather than reading it. Studies show that research productivity comes from personal characteristics as much as from ambition: some people like research and publication, and are good at it; others don't, and aren't. However, with career- and salary-promotion processes tied to publication, it is hardly surprising that greater emphasis is placed there.

In some cases, faculty members write papers that are presented at conference sessions attended by very people, and publish them in journals few people read and even fewer use. It is fair to ask if the money spent in these areas is worthwhile. Of course, the argument goes, the great work floats to the surface and becomes widely known; the rest is intellectual overburden, funded for the same reason that mining companies will dig dozens of holes before finding a bonanza.

It is time to rebalance the system. The country needs to support top, truly innovative researchers and maintain world-class capabilities in areas of interest and import to Canada. Cutting-edge research is as valuable now as ever, particularly when properly presented and widely shared. But we also need teaching-intensive faculty, the increasingly rare breed one finds in the office five days a week, meeting with students, sponsoring departmental activities, and creating the academic and social atmosphere of the engaging campus. The best teachers keep up with the literature and remain well-versed in their discipline; they simply find true pleasure sharing their knowledge with students.

There is a final category—the scholarship of synthesis—that holds the key to future learning and university impact. Given the proliferation of research, interpreters and sifters are needed. These scholars, among the rarest of academic birds, work their way through vast quantities of scholarship and find trends, innovations, and connections. In a world awash in ideas and insights, individuals who can wade through the material and share general insights with other scholars or external audiences are real treasures.

For forty or fifty years, teacher-scholars played a vital role, and served society, the university system, and themselves very well. But the time for the primacy of the teacher-scholar has passed. Universities need to celebrate and reward the accomplishments of teachers and scholars of synthesis more than they do at present. The result could well be less research, greater understanding, and more effective training and mentoring of the universities' students.

61   A Teacher's Lament

A visiting speaker from Japan, giving an excellent lecture on the continuing importance of industrial activity in the new economy, looked out at a sea of vacant stares and clearly uninterested students. At the end of the talk he said sadly, "It was like hitting golf balls into a fog. You cannot see anything land!"

A few years later, a professor was readying himself for the last lecture of the semester. It was also the day course assignments were due, and they had to be handed in during class time. Five minutes before class time only thirty of ninety students were in the lecture hall. In the last few minutes most of the rest arrived, walked to the front of the class, put their papers on the table by the podium—and left the room. One student arrived five minutes late, walked down the stairs to the front of the class right up to the professor (who was lecturing by that time), dropped the assignment and then double-timed it up the stairs and out of the classroom. Fewer than one-third of the students stayed for the lecture itself.

Some students may be surprised to learn that professors have feelings too. While a handful of profs put their class materials together hastily, most spend hours assembling lecture notes, readings, in-class exercises, and assignments. One colleague, lecturing in English, which is not her native language, estimates she spends ten to twelve hours preparing for each fifty-minute lecture—though hers is an extreme example. When students fail to show up for class, only play computer games, write emails during the lecture, or otherwise reveal their profound boredom, professors are understandably distressed.

Superstar professors—every campus has them—rarely have these problems. These exceptional teachers, gifted performers and wonderful communicators, are engaging, funny, emotional, and powerful. Their classes can be tours de force, remembered by students for years. Other brilliant teachers are more low-key, better known for their attention to student needs, their careful handling of course materials, and the careful construction and management of the class.

But many intelligent, reasonably competent, and likable teachers fail to make the top grade. And it is in their classes that the full impact of student disengagement is felt. These earnest and dedicated professors feel the pain of student uninterest—and worry about year-end teaching evaluations.

The front of the classroom can be a lonely place, where isolation grows with the size of the class. Professors are expected to entertain and inform, challenge and comfort, educate and inspire. If there is little feedback—and particularly if the students offer up blank stares, shuffling papers, eating, and other impolite distractions—time at the podium can be torture.

Some of our colleagues, including top-notch professors, suffer through their teaching. One used to throw up before almost every class. Another had a camp cot in his office on which he napped to recover after each lecture. Performing in a classroom takes a great deal out of a person. Just as a dynamic class can be energizing and exciting, an uninspiring class can be truly upsetting.

All professors want much the same thing. They want to educate. They want students to "get" the core information and ideas that form the foundation for future studies. Except for the weird ones—and there are a number of these—they care what the students think of them. They want their students to pursue additional courses in the field. More than anything, they want their students to take insights, ideas, theories, and concepts from the class and carry them out into the world and throughout their lives. Professors love their subject—they devote their lives to it—and are generally very excited about the course content.

Many classrooms, then, are the educational equivalent of giving a carefully chosen gift to a friend—and then to have her lose it, ignore it, or return it to the store for a refund. How demoralizing. Bored, disengaged, and disinterested students suck the intellectual vitality out of a classroom. They rob a wonderful opportunity of its potential and leave it dead on arrival.

62 It's Almost Impossible to Fire Profs

It's not totally impossible, but it's much more difficult than it ought to be. In the past profs usually lost their jobs due to political incorrectness—typically a prof with progressive political leanings running afoul of more conservative administrators. Frank Underhill, the University of Toronto historian, was almost fired in 1941 for predicting (correctly) that Canada would drift away from the British Empire and become more American. Harry Crowe did lose his job at United College (now the University of Winnipeg) in 1958 for criticizing the administration and particularly the role of the Presbyterian Church, which still ran the place in those days.

Today the main reason faculty members are fired is not for speaking their minds, but either for gross professional misconduct—the traditional offence is sexual activity with a student—or for flagrant violation of contract, an example being the physics prof at the University of Ottawa who was recently fired because he refused to grade his students, and when the administration insisted, gave them all an A+. A similar example was the prof at the University of Prince Edward Island who was suspended after he offered students a B– to leave his class, which he felt was overcrowded. These people bucked the system, but one thing that profs are never fired for is laziness and incompetence.

At most universities, faculty members are expected to teach, conduct research, and perform "service," which is usually a combination of committee work and other discipline-related activities inside and outside the university. Some institutions evaluate or review performance only at promotion time, which means that a person promoted to full professor at forty-five could work another twenty years without a further comprehensive review. Other places have annual or bi-annual reviews.

Whatever system is used, though, it's difficult—to the point of impossibility—to fire a seriously underperforming faculty member. The rules make it sound as though this were not true. The Queen's University collective agreement, for example, says that a tenured member may be fired for "gross misconduct, incompetence or persistent neglect of academic duties. Gross misconduct includes a pattern of serious misconduct." All of these terms are subject to interpretation, and of course a faculty member facing termination can appeal, launch grievances, go to the courts, and generally delay the process for years.

The main reason why terrible teachers can't be fired is that many universities have no really sound process in place for assessing them. Incompetence is difficult to prove. How do you prove that a prof is a bad teacher, when the only assessment is an annual form turned in by students answering questions such as "Does she seem to have a good grasp of the material?" Good luck going to court with that.

If a faculty member serves on a committee or two, preferably ones that meet only a couple of times a year, goes to a conference once in a while, writes a book review now and then, or copublishes a scientific paper with twenty other researchers, it's difficult to prove total neglect of duty. Add this to the years of paperwork involved and the hassles with faculty unions, and you can see why most administrators conclude that it's not worth the trouble to get rid of a bad apple or two. In truth, such apples make up only a tiny fraction of faculty members. Perhaps the system that makes it so hard to fire them is the price the universities pay to keep tenure safe. Too bad though, since it's the students and colleagues who suffer.

It's Hard to Get a Faculty Job

Professors have the best jobs around. The salaries are good, working conditions are superb, and flexibility is first-rate. Perhaps this is why they are among the hardest jobs to get in the country.

Think about what it takes to win the faculty job lottery. Start with a four-year undergraduate degree. Get high grades and perhaps a load of debt. Be one of the handful of students accepted to a first-rate Master's program. Ace the courses while applying for scholarships to pay the bills, and/or spend ten hours a week leading tutorials and grading papers. Cultivate professors for letters of reference for a PhD program at one of the top schools.

You got into Prestige University! Now your classmates are all as smart as you, and some are smarter. Keep studying—and never stop applying for grants. Struggle to make a name for yourself in the discipline by giving a few conference papers. If you are lucky your supervisor will help you publish an essay in a good journal. Work on your dissertation. Teach a course or two—you have to learn how sometime, and this is the place to do it. Three or four years pass. Graduate with your PhD.

Now you have a ticket to the big show, but you're not there yet. The universities have given out more tickets than there are seats in the professoriate. There are other jobs—in colleges, with government, and in the private sector—but by now you've been aiming for the big prize for ten years or more. Your professors tell you that you're one of the best. So you persist. You might apply for a post-doctoral fellowship, which will give you a year or two of research time and an opportunity to boost your publication list. But you are only putting off the inevitable job search.

You apply for jobs across the country (your own institution is probably off limits—universities aren't keen on hiring their own). There are a shockingly small number of places to approach. There was so much talk about retiring profs and a hiring boom that you figured you could pick and choose. Now, you just want something to apply for. Few of the jobs match your qualifications precisely, but a little fudging on the application letter doesn't hurt. You co-ordinate a mass letter-writing campaign in your support. If you're lucky, you'll make a shortlist at an acceptable university. For most, any invitation for a job interview will do.

Many of your friends will end up as "sessionals," teaching on limited term contracts for $35,000 a year. Some will only get a course or two and struggle to live on $15,000. They may do this for years, teaching courses for peanuts, few benefits, and no job security, until they get discouraged and quit.

But you are lucky—you get interviewed for a full-time job. The interviews are tough—a lecture to students, a presentation on your research, a tense meeting with potential colleagues, and a series of meals with members of the search committee. Then a long wait for a call from the department chair.

What are the odds you'll make it through? It's hard to be precise. In a few specialized fields—economics, electrical engineering, pharmacy, and accountancy—the success rate approaches 100 per cent. In most others, there are dozens of qualified applicants for every job on offer. In some fields—history, biology, philosophy, and physics—there can be several *hundred* top-notch candidates for a single post.

So you made it to a full-time, tenure-stream position at a Canadian university. Well done. You have landed in clover, caught the brass ring, won the lottery. True, you may be in your mid-thirties by this time, but compulsory retirement has been abolished, so enjoy it as long as your health holds out. Of course, you have to get tenure, and that can be scary, but almost everyone sails over this hurdle without difficulty. Welcome to the good life!

64 Your Prof Doesn't Take the Summer Off

One thing academics hate to hear the most is this: "It must be nice not to have to work for four months every summer!" Oh that it were so. It's true that profs don't teach in the summer (unless they are young and desperate for money), but almost all of them work surprisingly hard pretty much all year round.

It wasn't always that way. A couple of generations ago many university teachers did spend summers at the cottage, sometimes writing and thinking, but quite often just fishing. The majority never published a book or a major scientific paper—more than a few never published anything. But they were also badly paid, and had some moral right to take long holidays. Very few people do this any more: it would be a career-killer.

The formal workload of a university professor seems pretty easy. A full-time lecturer at a Canadian university will teach two semesters of thirteen weeks each. In the social sciences and humanities a standard teaching load involves three courses a week, three hours in the classroom for each. Scientists often supervise labs. Each hour of class time involves a certain amount of preparation and grading (more or less, depending on the availability of teaching assistants). So each course might involve eight hours of teaching time a week, for a maximum of twenty-four hours.

Many faculty members, though, teach two courses in one semester and three in the next, instead of the standard three and three, and big names can teach even less. But supervision of graduate students, if they have them, can be a huge drain on time. Faculty are also contractually required to do "service" to the university, which mostly means committee work, and since universities are largely self-governing, there is always a lot of this. Then there is the obligation to do research and scholarly publication.

Summer is the time when faculty members are supposed to conduct research, and most of them do, both because they like doing it and because promotion and salary raises largely depend on it. Scholarly work involves conducting research, attending conferences, writing up research results, grant proposals, articles and books, dealing with publishers, and so on.

It's a great life, so long as you value freedom more than money. There are two wonderful things about it. First, once a prof has tenure she is immune to hassles from above, so long as she fulfills her contractual obligations. Despite the alarms raised by faculty unions, the number of academics who have been fired in Canada for dereliction of duty over the past fifty years can probably be counted on the fingers of both hands (though some who went may have left when shown the writing on the wall). Second is flexibility. Profs can go to work late in the morning so long as they meet their classes, and they can head home early. They can work at home and can adjust their work schedule to accommodate family holidays. They can go to conferences in exotic places. As for research itself, either in a lab or an archive, it doesn't look that onerous to someone who sells real estate for a living.

Some faculty members whine about overwork, and a few waste time in university politics. But most realize how lucky they are to be doing what they love in an atmosphere relatively free of stress. In some ways it's the best job in the world: state funded (and therefore very secure), reasonably well-paid, with tons of flexibility, a great deal of self-direction, and a chance to make a difference—academic or practical—in the world. The overwhelming majority of the faculty realize this. They work hard with their students, on their classes, and on their research.

They are big users of email and stay in touch with professional colleagues around the world. Laboratory scientists are always on call and check in on their equipment regularly. Many contribute to social organizations, consult with governments, advise First Nations agencies, speak to community groups, write op-ed pieces, provide important context and background on the news, and otherwise contribute to making the city, region, and country better.

So professors don't take the summer off. Many work sixty to seventy hours a week and do so without much complaint. Professors work in a thousand different ways, and the overwhelming majority make real and sustained contributions. Just because they are not in their offices, and even though they are home at 3:30 p.m. to collect their kids from elementary school, they are still giving full value for their money.

Tenure Terror

Congratulations, newbie! You now work full time at a Canadian university. But your job is not yet secure. Looming ahead is the most stressful ritual of the academic profession: tenure.

The ability to speak openly about all manner of issues, comfortable or controversial, is the essence of a university. But fifty years ago, university professors did not have total freedom to profess. Those who offended the authorities—by criticizing church doctrine, speaking out on racial or cultural issues, or complaining about the administration of the university—could lose their jobs. Once in a while a prof with left-wing sympathies (alleged or actual) was fired, blacklisted, and otherwise mistreated.

Firings of university professors were not very common in Canada, but the possibility of dismissal cast a chill over the academy. So, how does a university protect faculty members while ensuring the quality and competence of the professoriate? The answer is tenure.

As you start out in your academic career you still have two significant hurdles to climb. First, there is a probationary review. Didn't we tell you? That first permanent contract was not permanent. You have to be reappointed to a second probationary term. If your teaching is not up to standard, if you are not fitting in well with colleagues, or if your research is weak the university can let you go at this stage. The option is rarely used, but it is a real and legal stage in the process.

As your fifth year is ending, you start preparing for the tenure application. This involves a statement about your research, teaching, and service activities; a departmental report on your contributions; and the selection of academic experts at other universities who can comment on your career. Your department will then review your file, sending its recommendations to a faculty-wide committee that makes a recommendation to a university committee, and then to the president for a final decision. It's cumbersome, but that's the way universities work.

If the final decision is unfavourable you are out. Most universities give you a last year of employment to sort out your affairs, but tenure denial means the loss of a job. You can try to find another one, but you are marked as a loser. Get turned down for tenure at one school and you could be out of the field forever. Pass the tenure bar and you are in for life. This is one big decision!

Tenure terror describes the long and stressful process leading up to the fateful decision. Junior faculty struggle to make sure they have met qualifications that are never entirely clear. Publish enough papers—but how many are "enough"? Get enough research grants—but how many? Teach well. Be a good colleague. Show potential. Make a difference professionally. And in the tenure year, sit on pins and needles while department, faculty, and university committees sit in judgment as you wait for the puff of white smoke that means you have passed the second greatest hurdle in your career (the first being to get the job in the first place). If the decision is negative you can appeal through your faculty association/union, but winning tenure this way will leave a nasty taste in your mouth for decades.

The good news for profs is that very few Canadian academics are denied tenure. It's different in the United States, where a substantial percentage of applicants are turned down at the leading universities. At Harvard tenure review is a well-known blood sport with the bar set almost unreachably high—you've published two books, but are they *seminal* books? Happily for you, Canadian schools do not have such ridiculously high standards.

Canadians, after all, are nice folks. Here faculty members in difficulty are often eased out of their positions before the tenure process starts. Frank conversations with department chairs or deans warn that you may get turned down. Many take the hint and seek employment at another institution or a career outside the academy.

Tenure terror is very real. Junior faculty members, even first-rate ones, feel this fear. Knowing that your career hinges on a single decision, made behind closed doors by colleagues in your department and faculty, is nerve-racking in the extreme. If the vote is negative you are crushed. If it's positive, lucky you. You're virtually unfireable.

Your Professor Is Not Overpaid

Each year the province of Ontario releases a list of everyone employed by government-funded agencies who earns more than $100,000 a year. The list generates a feeding frenzy as journalists looking for a cheap hit decry the outrageous salaries of civil servants and the malignant growth of the fat-cat bureaucracy. It makes for good blood sport at the expense of civil servants, and who cares about them? Universities are included on the list, and university faculty are among the fastest to scour the list for signs of injustice—does that idiot down the hall really earn $2,000 a year more than I do? The president makes four times my salary! *Aux barricades!*

There's more madness than method in this ritual. The symbolic $100,000 figure was picked several years ago, and has not been adjusted since then. As a result the number of people earning this sum or more has increased dramatically—largely because of negotiated salary increases and standard progression through the ranks. The current figure is roughly comparable to a $70,000 annual salary at the time the annual salary data was started. Ironically, the update encourages salary growth, as people identify themselves as underpaid and use the information to press their employer for more money.

The number of university faculty members making more than $100,000 a year—check out business school salaries if you want your eyes to pop out—naturally raises questions about the size of university pay packets. Most people think university faculty members have a pretty cushy job, with many other benefits not available to most workers. Although this isn't wrong, we think that university professors are not overpaid and that university salaries are very much in line with comparable wages in the Canadian economy.

The high salaries paid to profs in business, law, and medicine are set by international market pressures. Since Canada has one of the best university systems in the world it's hardly surprising that elite universities in the United States, the United Kingdom, and increasingly, East Asia come looking for talent in this country. With these competitors offering well over $200,000 a year for top people in high-demand areas, Canadian schools either have to be competitive or accept mediocrity. Most Canadian schools can't pay top dollar and rely instead on faculty attachment to Canada and the country's quality of living to convince them to take a Canadian job.

Don't forget the investment that faculty members make before they secure a faculty position: an undergraduate degree, usually a Master's degree, a PhD degree, and several years as a low-paid post-doctoral fellow or sessional teacher. And most researchers pay a substantial portion of their research costs and professional activity throughout their careers—a fact that's often ignored. Most faculty do not secure a tenure-stream faculty position until they are in their thirties, a full half-decade later than those seeking regular professional positions.

Finally, we need to put faculty salaries into context. Most high school teachers start around $55,000. In ten years or so they have reached their maximum of $85,000, subject to future pay raises, and they are still in their early thirties. Teachers have much less training than a faculty member with a PhD and typically have spent much less money on their education. The average salary level for university professors is high, but it takes them twenty years to reach the rank of Full Professor. They won't pull level with a high school teacher until they are well into their forties. Faculty should not complain about their salaries—not very many do, off-campus anyway—but they don't need to be overly defensive. University faculty are paid what they are worth. Few give less and many give more than fair value for the money they earn.

67 The Days of Academic Conferences May Be Numbered

The Waikoloa Hotel on Hawaii's Anaeho'omalu Bay seems a strange place to discuss social, economic, and political developments of northern and remote regions, but it's a nice perk for academics with the Western Regional

Science Association escaping their campuses in mid-winter. As you might guess, more than one colleague has found beaches, whales, and orchids far more interesting than multi-paper sessions by earnest academics. Some show up for their sessions, but generally they spend more time with mai tais than with lectures. One tried to combine the two and fell off the podium.

This conference was not a total boondoggle. The sessions were superb, and many great ideas were exchanged. Other, more prestigious conferences failed to match this gathering for academic rigour and intellectual value. A recent gathering of 5,000 social scientists in a major American city was notable mainly for the meagre attendance at most sessions. Some panels attracted only a handful of audience members, rendering the whole exercise largely irrelevant. But, boondoggle or not, the days of these conferences may be numbered.

Academic conferences are a multi-billion-dollar industry. Almost all scholarly associations have annual meetings. In Canada the Congress of Learned Societies attracts more than 7,000 people to its two-week series of academic meetings. Journalists cruise the Congress looking for papers with silly-sounding topics, candidates for the "Ig Nobel" Prize. Large medical and scientific conferences provide researchers with access to the latest results from the best labs in the world. The key sessions are standing-room-only and produce newsworthy presentations on cutting-edge discoveries.

Other faculty members meet in tiny workshops of a dozen or fewer people to discuss very narrow and esoteric topics. Regardless of size, these meetings allow scholars to get together with researchers with similar interests and for the presentation and debate of the latest research.

So why are academic conferences unlikely to continue in their current form? First, cuts to institutional budgets are reducing faculty travel, so that participants will have to pay part or all of their expenses. Second, at some point university faculty—individually and then collectively—will step up to the climate-change plate by refusing to engage in carbon-heavy travel. Declining attendance accelerates very quickly—if fewer scholars attend, the event becomes less interesting to other faculty.

But the real threat is technological. Until now conferences have played a crucial role. Academics love to talk, and they need to talk. Researchers with new discoveries, or exciting interpretations, have to test their ideas with their peers. But new technologies are changing the dynamics entirely.

In some disciplines, researchers circulate draft papers electronically, getting feedback that helps them revise the paper. Video streaming, video-conferencing, and the rapid decline in the costs of satellite transmission make it much easier to converse without travel. Scholars can reach thousands instead of dozens through podcasts and videoposts distributed through iTunes and other such sites.

In other words, many of the benefits of conferencing no longer need costly travel. Indeed, new technologies greatly expand the reach of new ideas and opportunities for intellectual exchange, especially as the generation raised on iPods, BlackBerrys, instant messaging, and the Internet takes over the professoriate.

Conference travel is a real perk for professors, so we can expect ferocious resistance to change. And there are professional development and networking options that are not easily replicated electronically (although this is overstated). But over time scholarly discourse will go digital, and academic conferences will slowly recede, joining illustrated lantern-slide lectures in the recesses of academic memory. It won't be the same as the papaya breakfast at the Waikoloa, though.

68 The Surprising Future of Libraries

For the past decade, universities have been alert to the possibility that their libraries, in their traditional form, were destined to become relics of the past. It seems, however, that they were wrong. On most campuses, library usage is up, students rely more than ever on the professional librarians, and the needs and possibilities of the information age seem destined to make the libraries even more important in the future.

The advent of the digital age was supposed to kill university libraries, or at least to transform them out of all recognition. Students and faculty would gather data on line, tapping into a vast world warehouse of digital content for their research and writing assignments. Books would disappear, replaced by websites and e-books. Paper journals, long the staple of the academy, would be replaced by freely distributed e-journals. The libraries, mausoleums for books, were obvious anachronisms. These large buildings would be expensive warehouses, taking up space and attracting few students. Why would students go to the campus library when they could fire up their laptops and do their research without getting out of bed?

As predicted, the digital age has arrived. Google Books, the largest digital collection in the world, available for free on the Internet, had over 20 million books available as of 2010. Research tools allow students and faculty to examine huge collections in seconds, selecting items that they can often review on their computer and print for free. Universities subscribe to enormous digital libraries of e-materials. While books in the traditional format are still being published in large numbers—and they play a vital role in faculty merit and promotion processes—an increasing number of these volumes are also accessible on line, thus rendering the physical copy less valuable, if not disposable. Library users can access all of this material from anywhere on campus, residence rooms, homes, or any place with an Internet connection.

Given mass digitization, the arrival at universities of a digitally savvy generation, and major university commitments to computerization, it should have followed that the libraries would fall into disuse, their space used for other purposes, and their financial and human resources reassigned. But this did not happen. Libraries today are dynamic and much-used places. Professional librarians are busier than ever. The digital age has forced university libraries to reinvent themselves and, in doing so, they have emerged even stronger, serving as social and intellectual hubs in ways that few would have forecast ten years ago. Libraries have been transformed from hushed places into active and vibrant learning spaces. Many of them have capitalized on the success of the Chapters bookstore model, adding coffee bars, comfortable chairs and, horror of horrors, they permit conversation! Where the university libraries used to consist of little more than hundreds of yards of book stacks, study carrels, and a few tables in reference rooms, they now have places for group work, computer facilities, and a wide variety of technical services. The "Learning Commons" idea has become particularly popular, providing large, open, and flexible spaces where students interact with each other and with professional staff.

Professional librarians are more valuable than ever. The so-called "digital natives"—young people educated in the digital age—are actually not very proficient in the use of online collections. They have become accustomed to quick and simple searches—a fast look at Google.com and a check of *Wikipedia* sources—searches that fall short of the standards of academic research projects. The proliferation of research collections, many times larger than standard university libraries, search tools designed to access newspapers and magazines, vast data sets of statistics and analytical data, and multi-lingual websites and documentary collections produce a diversity of sources that is well beyond the capability of an untrained undergraduate. Librarians have become information navigators, adept at finding data in digital haystacks and particularly skilled at training students in making full use of the library's holdings.

The predicted demise of the university library was premature. We live in an age of mass information, with huge quantities of government, academic, and public data coming available each year. Libraries have become even more essential, not less so, in the development of skilled researchers and analysts, something the students themselves have figured out. Visit a university library. Grab a cappuccino and a muffin, and head for the Learning Commons. Consult a librarian, and discover the pleasure of living in the information age.

Faculty Unions

Why on earth do faculty need unions? Far removed from the worlds of Norma Rae, the Wobblies, or the Canadian Auto Workers, faculty members have what the Chinese call an "iron rice bowl"—life-long jobs, career decisions made primarily by colleagues, excellent salaries, tremendous fringe benefits (including funded sabbaticals), a great deal of flexible time, and lovely working conditions. It's hard to imagine there's much left to fight for. The idea of faculty forming a union and going on strike for major improvements must seem ridiculous to most Canadians. More than a few university administrators think the same thing.

But you can make a good argument that the unions are necessary. Any large group of employees needs and deserves standardized arrangements, with some flexibility based on performance and competitive considerations. Those few places without formal faculty unions have faculty associations that perform almost all the same functions—they just don't have a legal right to strike. Universities cannot deal independently with hundreds of employees; they require structure as much as the faculty members do. There are hundreds of complexities in the work place—from harassment policies to appeals of tenure decisions—that require formal arrangements. Universities could, in the absence of a union/association, impose the rules, but they would pay a high price in terms of confusion, overlap, and faculty unhappiness. Likewise, salary negotiations would be incredibly difficult without the constructive (or occasionally, less than helpful) intervention of faculty representatives.

Faculty associations and unions are enormously helpful in resolving the often-intense personnel matters that arise in an employee-centric environment like a university. The vast majority of troublesome cases are handled through behind-the-scenes negotiations, and not through formal grievance and appeal procedures. Indeed—and contrary to the popular view of faculty unions—unions and associations are often just as stalwart in the defence of academic quality and professional conduct as the administration. Conflicts typically happen over process: Was a decision made in a manner consistent with natural justice and the existing faculty union/association agreement with the university?

Serious conflicts are surprisingly rare at Canadian university campuses. Strikes, which can be as nasty as any workplace confrontation, are noteworthy largely by their absence. Faculty members go to the wall only in exceptional circumstances and when they are extremely angry at the administration. Some of these conflicts have been memorable. In the late 1990s, a Maritime university facing the loss of an entire semester took drastic action. Rather than have the students lose their semester (and the university lose its money), the senior administration offered to set and mark final examinations for all students in all courses—and threatened to lock out the faculty for an additional four months. The faculty caved.

In recent years, most of the harshest conflicts have erupted between the administration and contract teachers and graduate students. The latter two groups feel—with justification—that they are being overworked and underpaid. Expect conflicts of this nature to expand in the coming years, as the teaching burden continues to shift to those without the security of tenure.

Tenured faculty members are treated extremely well—deservedly so—and they need unions or associations to represent their complex and often competing interests. But when they step over the line towards worker solidarity and the rhetoric of labour protest they sometimes find themselves in a different situation than their brothers and sisters on the factory floor and in the mining camp. They may not always elicit sympathy for their cause. The faculty association at a New Zealand university once called its members out on a one-day protest over stalled salary negotiations. Someone had the bright idea to dress up in academic regalia and solicit support along the major routes entering the university. Placard-carrying faculty members decked out in their university finery attracted a vigorous response—people driving by gave them the Kiwi equivalent of the finger. Not exactly the solidarity they had hoped for.

The Shame of the Sessionals

The Canadian university system has developed into a class system. At the top of the food chain are the research professors (holding Canada Research Chairs or endowed chairs), who teach very little and can do pretty much what they want with their time. In the middle are the majority of the professors, holders of tenured or tenure-stream faculty positions. At the bottom is an ever-growing army of casual, part-time, contract lecturers—often described as sessionals—who focus on undergraduate teaching and who get neither ongoing support for research nor job security.

Sessionals, hired to fill in gaps in departmental teaching requirements, were originally graduate students. Some had completed their PhDs and were either working on post-doctoral fellowships or in a holding pattern waiting for a full-time position. Some were well-qualified and well-trained individuals who just wanted to work part time. Teaching a course or two did not provide much money, but it helped. For people just entering the profession it was a good way to gain experience and put a couple of notches on their resume. (Some sessionals are experts in a field hired from the community to teach a course: lawyers, accountants, or artists—but these people are generally not teaching out of a dire need for money, and are not the ones we are concerned with here.)

Here's how it works. Professor X is going on a year's sabbatical. The usual arrangement is that she takes a 20 per cent pay cut. She's fairly senior and makes $125,000 a year, so she goes away on a $100,000 salary for that year. She usually teaches four one-semester courses, but only one has to be taught the year she's gone. The university hires a sessional for $6,000 (that's at the low end—at some places they make twice that per course). She gets her leave, a sessional gets hired, and the university saves $19,000. Everyone's happy.

But here is another, more modern scenario. Professor Y is retiring. He also makes $125,000 a year, but teaches five one-semester courses. His university wants all five courses taught. It could hire five sessionals, pay them $6,000 each, and save $95,000. Or it could hire one "full-time sessional" and pay her $35,000 to $50,000, depending on the institution. Often she would teach not five, but six courses for this salary. The higher course load is justified by the fact that the sessional is not expected to do research or sit on committees, just teach.

See how appealling this is to the university administration? The same number of courses are taught, or even more, and the administration saves thousands of dollars. And if you can save that much on one retirement, imagine how much you can save on ten, or thirty. The upshot is that universities increasingly hire sessionals, especially to teach first- and second-year courses, resulting in a two-tiered faculty, where the lucky tenured ones teach a few senior courses for a high salary, and the junior, untenured ones teach lower division courses for a pittance.

The *Socialist Voice* calls them "a flexible, underpaid, university proletariat," which is exactly what they are. They are usually hired on limited-term contracts, often a course at a time or for a single semester or year, so that the university does not become obliged to hire them permanently and does not have to pay benefits. One unnamed Canadian university reported that half its undergraduate English courses were taught by sessionals.

It can be a horrible life for a young academic, teaching a year or two here, another year there, or cobbling together two or three courses at different places—a morning course at Trent in Peterborough, say, and an afternoon course at Toronto's Scarborough campus. In an extreme case, a professor on the prairies taught fifteen separate sections of math in a single year—primarily the first-year math class—at four different institutions. People actually maintain these balancing acts, hoping to get on the tenure ladder, working without pension or other benefits and without access to the research grants needed to make big advances in their academic career. It's tough to get out of what an official of the Canadian Association of University Teachers calls an "academic ghetto," because people are hired for tenure positions largely on research, and full-time sessionals rarely have the time or money to do much of that. Some people toil in this ghetto for years before getting discouraged and finding another career.

There is another issue here, rather more delicate in nature. Universities brag about the number of tenure-stream faculty members teaching undergraduate classes; *Maclean's* annual university rating issue has made this a marker for commitment to excellence. But do the students care? It's hard to say, but anecdotally students are just as impressed with sessional instructors as they are with full-time professors. There are great and mediocre teachers in each group, the major difference being that poor sessional teachers are rarely invited back. Off they ride into the wilderness in search of another short-term, ill-paid appointment.

It's a bad, exploitive situation, and it's going to get worse. Universities continue to overproduce PhDs in many fields (while underproducing in others, but few history scholars want to switch to finance or electrical engineering). A huge infusion of government money would allow universities to staff up, eliminating both the need for so many sessionals and the tiny fingerhold that thousands of sessional faculty have on an academic career. Government funding of that scale is not going to happen, nor are tenured faculty likely to fill the need by teaching more. Increasingly, sessionals themselves have taken action by unionizing. In the meantime, shame on government and the universities for permitting this situation to continue.

The Strange Economics of Scholarly Publishing

Every February Canadian writers, academics among them, look for a special envelope—the annual cheque from the Public Lending Rights Commission. This is a government-funded organization that supports Canadian writers. Every year it polls ten secretly selected libraries. Every time your book appears you get about $30 (it varies year by year). If the book is in all ten libraries you get $300; if you have ten books in ten libraries you get $3,000 (the maximum permitted). Access Copyright, a similar program, provides payments for writing copied for distribution and use. This program pays for use of scholarly journals, among other publications.

For academics, whose royalties from university presses, as we know only too well, would hardly buy a case of beer, and are more often nothing after a year or two, the PLR payment is like manna from heaven. It is also one of the only bright spots in an otherwise dreary scholarly publishing world.

Scholarly publishing is a strange enterprise. Academics don't publish for direct financial benefit—or if they do, they are almost always disappointed. But the indirect returns, in the form of merit pay, outstanding performance bonus, and promotion, can be considerable. If faculty members tell you they don't make any money from publishing, don't believe it! A good publishing year can produce early promotion and a permanent salary increase of $1,000 or more, paid out for the rest of the faculty member's career, factored into pensions. So a book published early in a career could be worth $50,000.

This explains why university teachers are willing to publish in journals that have "page charges"—that is, the author has to pay the publisher so many dollars per page. We've never done it, but it's common in the sciences.

Scholarly journals/magazines typically fall into two groups: journals produced and subsidized by academic associations and those produced by for-profit companies. The latter are particularly important in the scientific and medical fields. In certain areas—neuropsychology but not Canadian history, biochemistry but not English literature—the journals are incredibly expensive and produce substantial profits for their owners. How expensive? A subscription to the journal *Brain* costs close to $1,000 a year. Universities have tried unsuccessfully to break the dominance of the biggest journal publishers, but professors' desire to publish in these prestigious journals has limited the effectiveness of these efforts.

Canadian academic book publishing operates in a similarly odd way. Few trade (for-profit) publishers produce academic books, and then usually only from marketable "star" quality academics such as John English, Mark Kingwell, Thomas Homer-Dixon, Frances Westley, and Richard Florida. A small number of university presses produce the vast majority of Canadian scholarly books. Book prices are a real deterrent to the general public and dampen whatever market enthusiasm is left—even for books written in accessible prose.

Academic work focuses on the production and publication of scholarly research. Because of government and university support, the profit motive doesn't enter into the equation. Little effort is devoted to pursuing readership among academics and even less among the general public. The university system produces ever more articles and books, most of which attract very few readers or purchasers. The scholarly writing has much less impact than the system assumes and wants. Many words are printed. Not all are read.

PhDs Don't Drive Taxis

If they do, they are either conducting some sort of research, seeing how the other half lives for a while, or their careers have hit a titanic iceberg. In general though, the taxi driver with the advanced degree is a pretty rare phenomenon. Even someone who has earned a PhD in a field where job prospects are tiny—say, a degree in Classical Greek Literature with a dissertation on Aristophanes' *The Frogs*—will likely not have to take such a stressful, ill-paying job.

The taxi cliché (academics call this a "meme") is really just a stand-in for the idea that there are highly educated people who can't get the jobs they were educated for, and thus, by extension, university degrees are a waste of time and money. There's some truth to this. It can be very difficult for a PhD to get a PhD-level job, but there's a big difference between lowering your sights somewhat and driving a taxi.

In 2001, the average total lifetime income of working Canadians with different levels of education was as follows, though the difference seems to have declined since then:

Grades 9 to 11	$1.07 million
High school diploma	$1.18 million
College diploma	$1.36 million
Bachelor's degree	$2.15 million

It's obvious what a huge advantage having an undergraduate degree makes in many, though not all cases. But it seems that having a PhD does not give a big salary advantage over a Master's. A 2007 survey of Canadians holding graduate degrees, taken two years after graduation, found that while people with Master's degrees earned $60,000, those with doctorates earned only $5,000 more. Considering how much longer it takes to get a PhD, and how much debt graduates sometimes take on, it hardly seems worth the effort, from a financial point of view.

Undergraduate degrees often do pay off in terms of lifetime income. Young people know that, which is a main reason they go to university. For graduate degrees, however, the financial gain is less clear. A PhD gets her first steady job in her thirties, while a high school teacher of the same age has been working for ten years and is near the top of the salary ladder. You don't get a PhD to get rich—the rewards are not monetary—but you rarely end up driving a taxi.

VII
Universities in Canadian Society

73 There's a New Quiet Revolution in Quebec

English-speaking students and professors visiting Quebec in the mid-1970s were often in for a rude shock. The province's university campuses were heavily radicalized, having provided the intellectual direction and passion behind the Quiet Revolution and the rise of the separatist movement. Now they are at it again, but in a very different way. Quebec's universities are playing a key role in the economic transformation and competitiveness of the provincial economy, and have made themselves a force to be reckoned with in the international university landscape.

The new-look Quiet Revolution is markedly different. Gone are the flamboyant speeches, but the fiery nationalism survives. The new revolution is based on the belief that Quebec and the Quebecois can compete economically, and that they can do so without surrendering their souls to English-speaking political parties or companies. The battlefield has shifted, too, from history and political science departments—surprisingly, even disappointingly, quiescent in recent years—to the business schools and some of the leading technology centres.

The new Quebec is something to admire. Assertively Quebecois, but comfortably bilingual, French-Canadian students and researchers are much less radicalized than thirty years ago. Many Quebecois students attend English-language institutions, graduates move easily in Canadian and international business environments, and universities play a vital role in regional and provincial development.

Montreal is one of the richest academic-community environments in North America, with a wonderful slate of first-rate institutions: McGill, Université de Montréal, Université de Québec à Montréal, Concordia University, and the underrated École Polytechnique. Laval University in Quebec City is a fine university, no longer as highly rated internationally as U de M and McGill, but still one of the best humanities and social science universities in North America.

Where Quebec universities really stand out—aided, it must be said, by aggressive provincial government involvement—is in the development of the provincial economy. Montreal has emerged as a Canadian leader in pharmaceuticals and aerospace. Sherbrooke (only recently an industrial dinosaur) has shown great creativity and determination, led by the Université de Sherbrooke. Quebec City, backed by Laval's strong commitment to provincial evolution, is emerging as a creative and high-technology centre. HEC Montreal (formerly the École des Hautes Études commerciales de Montréal) is one of the most impressive and active business schools in Canada, highly regarded internationally and with superb business connections inside the province. The MBA programs at HEC consistently rank among the top in North America and internationally. Almost a third of their students are international—an illustration of how Quebec business programs are leading the province into the global economy.

Quebec's last revolution was very noisy, and the impact of the rise of Quebec separatism still reverberates across the country. This new revolution is subtle and yet equally transformative. Quebec is forging a substantial presence in the national and international marketplace—Lavelin and Bombardier are just the best known of a group of impressive companies.

Provincial universities, the pride of Quebec's post-1960 renaissance, have maintained a crucial role in this latest recasting of the province's place within Canada and the world.

Academic Freedom is Endangered by Neglect

It has been fifty years since there was any real assault on academic freedom in Canada. Why, then, worry about it now? Because it's an issue that is never totally settled. Over the past two years, the Canadian Association of University Teachers (CAUT) has provoked debates about academic freedom on several campuses. CAUT is concerned about the possibility that donor agreements give benefactors the ability to interfere in faculty hiring and academic programs, matters which they argue are the exclusive preserve of university faculty and institutional procedures. The pages of the CAUT *Bulletin* provide ample evidence about the recent controversies at Waterloo, Wilfrid Laurier, Ottawa, Carleton, and York. These debates have consumed a large amount of institutional time, forced Carleton to redraft an agreement, and led to the cancellation of a major donation to York. However, these are far from being the most important battlegrounds for academic freedom in Canada.

Most of the current debate within universities is fairly moderate, perhaps because the biggest battles are behind us: issues relating to feminism, indigenous rights, sexual identification/orientation, and racism—though not completely resolved—have been substantially addressed. Similarly, the once-radical cry for environmental awareness is now a widely accepted maxim of mainstream society. Despite these dramatic changes, many aspects of contemporary society remain in need of informed and critical commentary.

Faculty members rightly insist on the ability to research controversial topics and to offer radical ideas, even ones that are profoundly disturbing to the public at large. This is one of the key responsibilities of the university. Faculty need the right to research what they want, publish what they can, and say what they can defend. But this right carries an obligation to engage, to share ideas, and to risk the criticism that attends controversy. Canadian universities offer strong protection for academic freedom. So does the *Charter of Rights and Freedoms*. Unfortunately, most Canadian academics have not exercised this powerful right and responsibility as fully as they should.

There are, of course, some Canadian scholars who express controversial views in public (take, for example, three examples from Alberta: Frances Widdowson of Mount Royal University, Tom Flanagan of Calgary, and Anthony Hall of Lethbridge, all of whom have expressed provocative views on Aboriginal policy among other issues). While we might disagree with many of their ideas, we most certainly applaud their willingness to hold unpopular opinions.

So here is a radical idea. Canada needs more—not less—academically driven controversy. We need scholars who are writing and speaking from positions of academic knowledge and insight to challenge the system. We need informed, engaged, and prompt academic intervention on all of the major issues of our time. We need to acknowledge that very few controversies leap from the pages of peer-reviewed academic journals and university press books (there have been some of each, of course). While there are some public intellectuals in Canada who are adept at bringing challenging new ideas to public discourse, we need many more of them. Scholarly research and professional understanding has to reach society at large to have a real and immediate impact. Faculty members need to reflect on the possibility that our quiet, non-controversial approach to national and international issues is a serious threat to academic freedom—or at least is a missed opportunity for faculty members to make a difference in Canada and the world.

Language Study Is in Decline

Full disclosure: one of us cannot speak another language and has only a scanty reading knowledge of French. The other is more proficient and has enough of several other languages to at least sound erudite. We share a belief, however, in the fundamental importance of language instruction and of gaining the cultural understanding that goes with knowing another language, to say nothing of the economic advantages.

Until fairly recently, proficiency in a second language (almost always French for Anglophones) was a requirement for high school graduation and university admission everywhere in Canada. It still is in many places. Being competent in a language other than English was a key sign of an educated and cultured mind, one of the things that "every educated person should know."

Times have changed. Latin, German, and Greek are all but dead in the public high school system. University course enrolments in these languages are also down sharply across Canada. There is no royal road to mastering another language, and, leaving aside French immersion, fewer students these days are willing to make the necessary effort to do so. Besides, many argue, English has become the global language (four years ago there were 300 million Chinese studying our language), removing the need for Canadian students to expand their studies beyond French. The closure or amalgamation of foreign-language (that is, other than English or French) programs and departments at universities has become depressingly commonplace.

True, plenty of students are studying Asian languages, but the steady growth of these classes, especially Chinese and Japanese, has been dominated by students of Asian ancestry. Students who grew up with Chinese can make a much faster adjustment to Japanese, and vice versa, than students raised speaking only English or French. To make matters worse, it seems that Canadian companies rarely value foreign-language ability and cultural understanding. Graduates of foreign-language programs do not find employers beating a path to their doors. The incentive to learn another

185

language has to be personal more than financial.

The loss, to the students and to Canada, is considerable. Students who learn another language improve their own. Those who don't are missing the cultural insights that accompany mastery of another language. And they lose the capacity to function comfortably in other countries and societies.

Canadians, who constantly boast about our multicultural character, have a limited capacity to speak to each other, let alone to the rest of the world. We pale by comparison to northern Europeans, for example, and share only with the United States the deep cultural myopia of unilingualism. Is it better that 300 million Chinese speak English than that a substantial number of Canadians speak Chinese? We don't think so. Sadly, intellectual laziness and cultural blinders mean that the problem of language learning is only going to get worse.

Successful Universities Need a Ton of Money

Governments provide a ton of money to universities. Annual per-student grants, building funds, indirect costs of research payments, and specialized research awards attract lots of attention. But actual government expenditures on universities go far beyond this, and may be 30 to 40 per cent higher than most Canadian realize. Much of this hidden expenditure, surprisingly (or not, for the realist), goes in the form of payments to the upper-middle-class and the wealthiest Canadians. Here's how it works:

Example One: Donors to Canadian universities get tax receipts for their donations. At the most basic level, a cash donation reported on an individual return, donors receive a percentage of their donation back in the form of a tax refund. A $10,000 donation is actually made up of $7,000 in private cash and $3,000 in public funds.

Example Two: Recently the government changed the regulations governing the donations of shares to charities, including universities. Someone who bought shares at $1 and sold them years later for $100 a share would pay capital gains tax on the $99 per share difference. Under the new rules, if an individual donates the shares to a charity, such as a university, she pays no capital gains tax but gets a tax receipt for the full $100 value of the shares. The actual impact depends on an individual's tax situation, but the rules essentially mean that the government is foregoing about 40 per cent in lost taxes. In effect it is allowing the donors to direct those "taxes" to the charity of their choice. This reduces the net cost of the donation to the donors—they get public credit for the full value—and the government is again supporting the university (or other charity).

Example Three: Elsewhere we discuss the manner in which low tuition fees, tuition deductibility (typically by the parents), and tax-protected educational savings plans (with a nice federal grant on top of the personal contribution) represent a major subsidy for wealthy Canadians. They are also subsidies for the university, for they encourage a higher level of university attendance than would be the case if students had to pay a higher percentage of the cost. For the wealthy, these government arrangements can cover half or more of the cost of attending university. For the poor, the impact is negligible.

Example Four: Towns and cities love universities. They lend "class," and are a draw for employers. In return, the municipalities provide some nice financial support, either in the form of property-tax-free status, contributions equal to all or most of the taxes, or investments in university infrastructure. These arrangements can run into millions of dollars a year, a healthy bonus for the institution.

Example Five: Student loans seem like a fair deal for the taxpayer, for they have repayment plans built into them. But remember two things. First, students pay no interest on the loans until six months after they graduate—another silent subsidy. In 2007, there were just under a million student borrowers, with a total debt to the government of more than $8 billion—a good chunk of it interest-free money. Second, the default rate on loans for university and college students is more than 15 per cent (private college students 25 per cent more than public). Governments surrender millions of dollars to students who default ($70 million as long ago as 1996–97), often to students who failed to complete their studies. For taxpayers, this is another indirect subsidy for colleges and universities.

Successful universities require a great deal of money, and we have no problem with government support for the enterprise. There are major gaps, however, in public knowledge about the extent of government subsidies, tax concessions, and other means of support. People know governments provide a lot of money for universities. Little do they know how much.

Universities Need Core Courses

The idea of core—compulsory across the board—courses is the other issue (besides athletics) on which the authors have a major disagreement. One of us thinks they are a fine idea; the other, though not denying this, thinks that, given our universities' hunger for students, core courses simply won't work. We invite the reader to judge our cases. This chapter puts forward the case for core courses, while Chapter 87 offers the contrary view.

Most Canadian universities have abandoned one of their main responsibilities. Many of their disciplines refuse to define what a well-educated, properly prepared undergraduate student should study and learn. Contrast two standard faculties: engineering and arts. In the former, and with the help of a vigilant professional association, incoming students are given a rigidly prescribed set of courses. The first year is generally completely fixed, with few if any elective courses. Faculties of arts are very different.

In Arts, students rarely enter with a defined major. Instead, they enter as intellectual free agents, able to sup freely at an academic smorgasbord. No constraints for arts students; they can take whatever they like. On the surface, the logic of the more open and flexible arrangement is compelling. Imagine telling incoming students, finally freed from the shackles of high school, that they have no choice in what they take. Incoming students do not want paternalistic faculty members telling them what to do. Indeed, why not open the world to them, and let them study whatever they like? Over a short time, the argument goes, they will explore the academic universe, develop an interest, and gain precisely the kind of broad, comprehensive education for which the liberal arts are known.

Unfortunately, the smorgasbord approach to first-year course selection does not serve a large number of students. Many students—it is impossible to be precise here—do not head off in a great intellectual treasure hunt, testing out new fields of endeavour and exploring new disciplines. Instead, most first-year students appear to follow a safe approach: study things they were good at in high school; avoid unnecessary and difficult science and math courses (goodbye math and physics; hello "rocks for jocks" and introduction to astronomy); and, take courses that promise to talk about sex (such as psychology or sociology).

Academic adventurism is fine when students are comfortable, well prepared, and confident. However, when students are unsure of themselves, it is a recipe for boring and safe choices, crowd-following, and work avoidance. That first-year course in Russian or Chinese seems a lot more daunting than sticking with familiar turf, such as first-year English, French, and biology. By giving students almost carte blanche to explore the academy as they see fit, however, universities simply re-enforce conservative and safe choices.

Core courses provide a partial solution to this situation. Universities know what students should learn and they know the kind of courses and programs of study that prepare them well for advanced years. They also know that the average seventeen- or eighteen-year-old is not likely to happen upon the right set of courses by chance. A proper first-year program lays out a sequence of required courses. Some of them may be comprehensive classes that introduce students to the range of disciplines within the academy. McMaster, for example, requires students to take a first-year course called "Inquiry," which canvasses many of the basic disciplines and provides a focused introduction to fundamental university-level skills. UNBC, at its founding, committed five first-year courses to a comprehensive review of the humanities, social sciences, natural sciences, physical sciences, and university communication. There are other variants around. The University of King's College in Halifax has a particularly successful one.

University students need and deserve guidance, particularly at the point of entry. There is no reason why all students cannot get a common core of foundational courses that will serve them well in later years. The University of Manitoba has taken this approach, delaying students' degree choices until they have a solid and full year of studies under their belts. Experimentation and wide-ranging choices require an understanding of options. Few first-year students really understand what sociology or anthropology are, let alone rhetoric, nanotechnology, media studies, communication, gerontology, gender studies, and many other interesting and emerging fields. Given students` general areas of interest, universities should tell them what they need to know and should provide a narrow set of courses that will provide them with the basic and fundamental skills required for academic success. Without core courses, first-year students are abandoned to nibble at the edges of new knowledge; with them, they can be introduced to a deep and thoughtful understanding of the intellectual range of the modern academy.

Academic Fraud Is a Reality

Universities need to be vigilant. This means more than being on the lookout for violations of academic integrity (a nice way of saying "cheating"). The academy is surrounded by a minefield of fraudulent credentials, fake degrees, and misrepresentation of academic achievements.

In the era of the Internet, where it is quite easy to check on the claims made by public figures, it has become commonplace to discover political candidates and high-profile figures who have overstated their university accomplishments and claimed degrees that they did not earn.

Applications from abroad can pose a particular problem, though most are honest. Institutions receive thousands of applications a year from many nations, from private and public schools, from major centres and little-known towns. Staff in registrar's offices have to identify these institutions, assess them, and review the content of their courses. They then have to convert foreign grades into provincial equivalents to determine eligibility for admission. This takes an enormous amount of effort—some institutions contract out these reviews to private companies—but it is essential if institutions are to maintain their academic standards.

Even such scrutiny does not protect against fraud. In some countries, unscrupulous educational agents take money to ensure that a client's son or daughter gets into a top Canadian school. Sometimes the agent, or someone else, is involved in forging transcripts. Cleverly done—often in the language of the home country and therefore more difficult to verify—they can slip past even the careful review of the admissions clerks. Of course, students unable to succeed at university will fail soon enough, but this is hardly an effective line of defence against such cheating.

If students need a little illicit help once they've been accepted into university, it's easy to find. *The Chronicle of Higher Education* recently carried an article about a man who makes about $60,000 a year writing student papers—not just short undergraduate ones, but long pieces for graduate and professional students. He claims to have written a PhD dissertation in sociology and a Master's degree in cognitive psychology. It's available on-line, and makes for enlightening and depressing reading.

Want a prestigious degree from a top institution? Just include it in your resumé—and hope that no one checks. There's little chance they will. In the United States fewer than 20 per cent of employers ask to see university transcripts as part of the hiring process—even universities routinely fail to ask to see a copy of the record of grades and marks of people applying for jobs.

A psychology professor, hired on the basis of an impressive resumé, turned out to a complete fraud. A customer had left his resumé in the man's taxi and, using the document as leverage, the fraudster managed to get a full-time job at a small Canadian university, even though he'd never attended university at all. It took an entire semester to unmask him.

Another individual, eager to find work, submitted her husband's resumé as her own to a competition and was awarded a position. As with the psychology professor, who kept talking about "maniac depressives," it was the students who detected her ignorance. Their complaints led to investigations and, eventually, firing.

Fake degrees are widespread around the world, offered through paper institutions that exist only to collect payments and issue diplomas. Other institutions, particularly in the United States, offer degrees on very specious grounds—those that give credit for "life experience" and award a degree for a couple of months' work are particularly popular. One western Canadian professor drew attention to his PhD degree when applying for promotion. A member of the committee checked out the institution that had awarded it, and discovered that it was little more than a mail drop. The faculty member claimed to have been in full-time study for a period of time that overlapped with a summer teaching commitment at another institution. He offered to bring in a copy of his thesis to prove he had earned his degree. Sadly, there was a fire in his garage that week and his documents were lost. He wasn't fired, but he wasn't promoted.

Given the number of universities and colleges in the world—more than 17,000—it's impossible for universities or employers to know about all of them. The very diversity of the system creates openings for fraud. Many of those peddling false information, either to get into an institution or to attract attention and interest in the workplace, will be caught out. When they are discovered, action tends to be decisive and harsh. After all, university degrees are ephemeral and intangible products—the reputation comes from the collective accomplishments of the students and faculty. Trying to gain credibility by association, or trying to claim academic achievements where none exist, undercuts the integrity of the whole system.

Guaranteeing Basic Competencies

The student's email was gracious, including glowing comments on her experience at the university, giving her professors full credit for her acceptance into a prestigious graduate school. It was, in all respects save one, the kind of letter that gets circulated widely as a celebration of the faculty's success. The "but" is significant. The email was four paragraphs long and had at least twenty-five grammatical and spelling mistakes. It was, as an example of a graduate's ability to communicate at an advanced professional level, a real embarrassment.

Universities make strong statements about the benefits of an academic degree. Graduates, we promise, will be able to read and write effectively. They will have strong analytical skills, be able to defend their ideas, speak clearly, conduct advanced research using primary and secondary sources, and (in some disciplines) be numerate and able to handle statistical material. It is a long and impressive list, well connected to the skills that employers declare essential for career and personal success.

What we should be saying is that university students have a chance to *gain* these basic competencies, not that they will necessarily *have* these skills when they graduate. Virtually all programs have classes and assignments that test and improve students' general abilities—as well as adding specialized knowledge and discipline-specific skills. Chemistry students learn to work in highly technical laboratories; historians gain insights into how to conduct primary research. Both groups of students should learn to read, write, and participate in debate about disciplinary ideas and concepts.

Alas, the truth is that many students graduate without strong abilities in the core skill areas. In one particularly egregious case, a mature student failed a number of courses (she was required to withdraw from the university on several occasions) until she found professors who were easy graders and didn't care much about writing skills. She took every course they offered, gradually earning enough credits for an Associate's degree (the equivalent of two years' study). She still could not write.

193

With growing class sizes, increased use of part-time instructors, strains on student support services, and heavy demands on professors, universities are not always able to give individual students the focused attention they require. The decline in admission standards at many institutions has also meant that a significant number of students enter universities without the traditional set of academic skills.

Universities must ensure that a degree conveys a specific message about their graduates. Holding a degree from a publicly funded Canadian university should mean that a graduate has each of the basic core competencies at an appropriate level. An English major's numeracy skills may be much lower than a computer science graduate's, but the English student will certainly have far more advanced abilities in literary analysis. Individual programs and faculties should make clear and public commitments to ensuring that these core competencies are taught in a series of required courses. These courses—whether they ask the student to demonstrate appropriate writing, analytical, presentation, or other skills—should operate as gatekeepers for the degree, ensuring that each graduate of the program has the abilities that the university, faculty, and department/program have identified as being integral to it.

Establishing the core competencies, program by program, is a contentious but necessary task. Assigning courses that ensure students have the required, specific skills will be difficult. Equally, universities will have to offer remedial assistance to students who are otherwise doing well in their program but who founder on one of the fundamental requirements. With core competencies defined and embedded in academic programs, and with extra help for students struggling to get over a specific bar, the quality of graduates and the meaning of a university education will improve considerably. A first step involves having a few words with professors who don't care much about writing skills.

A small-business owner called two years ago to complain about a recently hired graduate from the university. This young person had been hired because of his supposed ability to operate in his native language and in English. The position required English-speaking and writing abilities. The student had difficulty making himself understood in English, particularly on the telephone, and could not write at a professional level. "What," asked the employer, "does a degree from your university mean if a graduate cannot handle the most basic of all tasks?" It is a fair question—and one that requires urgent and system-wide attention.

80 A Nationally Uneven System

Ontario, for decades the wealthiest province in Canada, has long been parsimonious with universities. Few people know that Ontario ranks tenth out of ten provinces in funding for universities per student. Expressed on a North American scale (fifty states and ten provinces), Ontario ranks fifty-ninth.

What? A wealthy province, with a set of superb research-intensive universities and a network of access-based institutions, ranks lower than Prince Edward Island and Manitoba, and slums with Mississippi near the bottom of the continental rankings? It should be embarrassing, but no one seems embarrassed.

Here's the back story: Federal government equalization payments (until recently Ontario provided billions of dollars for redistribution to the other provinces) provide block funding to the provinces for education, health, and social services. Before the Trudeau era, this money was tied to specific activities and expenditures—so much for health, so much for universities. In 1977 Prime Minister Pierre Trudeau, in an ill-conceived act of appeasement to the provinces, put all of the money into a single pot called the "block funding transfer," and gave the provinces the power to spend it as they wished. The unchecked growth of healthcare spending subsequently ate up an ever-larger portion of this fund, leaving an ever-smaller portion for the university sector.

Provincial governments have different priorities, and they allocate their funds accordingly. The Atlantic provinces, led by Nova Scotia, truly believe in post-secondary education and have walked the talk. Ontario, despite lip service paid by Premier Dalton McGuinty to education and research, sits at the bottom of the pile, well behind big-spending, right-wing Alberta and right behind social democratic nanny state Quebec.

Here are the public funding figures for Canadian universities, per student, for 2007–2008 (source: Statistics Canada):

Alberta	$22,469
Saskatchewan	$18,067
Newfoundland and Labrador	$16,169
Manitoba	$13,860
Nova Scotia	$13,552
Prince Edward Island	$13,209
New Brunswick	$13,114
Canada (national average)	$12,500
British Columbia	$12,342
Quebec	$12,006
Ontario	$9,718

The implications here are huge. Dalhousie University, a fine Maritime school, has much smaller class sizes than the University of Waterloo—an equally fine institution but clearly very cost efficient. York University is starved for cash compared to places like the University of Manitoba or Simon Fraser University. The president of a large Ontario university (not Waterloo) observed that his budget would be almost twice the size if his institution were in Alberta. Over time—and Ontario's slide has been pronounced and increasing—the gap between the quality of education, research, and service between the provinces will get wider and wider.

What is odd about the differences between provinces is that they don't follow the standard Canadian pattern. The Atlantic provinces are not the poor children of the post-secondary system in Canada; Ontario holds that distinction. The Government of Ontario argues, with some justification, that the problem lies with the distribution of tax revenue in Canada. It is also true that the allocations reflect provincial priorities. Ontario's top priority is accessibility, not the quality of the educational experience. Equally, the province funds all institutions on the same per-student basis (there is more flexibility with research funding and capital budgets, the latter being closely tied in all provinces to political considerations). Canada is nothing if not committed to full equality.

The distortions are either offset or made worse by donor support and specialized government grants, depending on the success of fundraising drives. British Columbia funds capital projects separately from the per-student grants. Ontario occasionally has time-limited allocations for major buildings, but universities are also expected to pay for buildings through their annual budgets. The result—evident to anyone who visits campuses in the two provinces—is aesthetically pleasing buildings in British Columbia, functionality and frugality in Ontario.

For many decades, the distinctive characteristic of Canada's university system was its uniform quality. The University of New Brunswick is a terrific university, despite the province's lower standard of living. Alberta's long-term prosperity did not automatically ensure a better system. This pattern is now very much at risk, and significant changes are starting to show up. In this respect, Canada will be moving closer to the American model of public education, where there are substantial differences between and even within states. Given the nature of federal-provincial relations—and Quebec's jealous stranglehold on all matters educational makes significant changes extremely difficult—it is highly unlikely that a national solution will be found.

It's safe to say that the gap between rich and poor will accelerate and that differences based on quality and resources will increasingly become a feature of the Canadian university system. As we argue elsewhere, this is not necessarily a bad thing, but it's certainly not the traditional Canadian way of doing things.

Quebec's Funding Fiasco: Building Provincial Mediocrity

Quebec, even more than Alberta, is the classic Canadian outlier. It loves to do its own thing. And its universities are no exception. The province has a CEGEP system, essentially combining Grade 12 and first-year university into a transition program from high school to post-secondary studies. It maintains the only truly provincial network of universities—the Université de Québec, with ten campuses across the province. It supports both English and French institutions (as does Ontario, by the way, particularly through York University's Glendon College and the bilingual University of Ottawa and Laurentian University). But it is on the tuition front that Quebec really stands apart.

Under the influence of the powerful student and faculty unions, Quebec has resisted the temptation to increase tuition fees to keep up with rising university costs. Result: Quebec's university fees are the lowest in the country, around $2,000 per year for an Arts degree (for residents of the province) compared to a national average of around $5,000. The provincial government is ideologically wedded to the (very bad) idea of keeping university fees artificially low, believing it is central to its goal of achieving broad accessibility. When the province's leading business schools sought to raise their fees to allow them to compete—principally for top scholars—with English Canadian and American schools, the government closed off the option. The authorities even indicated that they would claw back from the government grant to the university any additional income earned from higher fees.

Quebec's low tuition fees have been a failure. The province has the second-lowest university participation rate in Canada, and by quite some distance. The provinces with the highest fees have the highest participation rates, a disquieting result that flies in the face of student and Quebecois assertions about the impact of tuition fees. So students get a cheap ride and threaten to take to the streets in protest at the slightest sign of tuition reform or increases. The provincial government—knowing only too well from the history of the post-1960 era the role of the academy in political protests and the separatist movement—is afraid to antagonize a potentially formidable foe. It opts for the easy solution, one that hamstrings Quebec institutions, subsidizes the wealthiest families in the province, and doesn't promote broad university participation.

But Quebec has allowed higher tuition fees in other areas. Again standing apart from Canadian norms the province allows the universities to charge higher fees for out-of-province Canadian students (and higher fees again for international students). A Montreal student enrolled at Concordia will pay $2,000 for a first-year Arts program; a student from Edmunston, across the border in New Brunswick, pays $5,600; and an international student pays $18,000. No other province charges higher fees for out-of-province Canadian students, for it undercuts one of the core principles of Canadian federalism: the transferability of social benefits. The policy has not raised any public outcry, largely because of the country's reluctance to stir up Quebecois reaction. It's outrageous, of course, but that's the kind of country we live in.

Quebec itself is the major loser here. Its fee structure is a significant disincentive for Canadians from other provinces. At a time when thousands of young Canadians graduate each year from French-immersion programs, you'd think Quebec would be delighted to welcome these French-speaking students to their province. Quebec's birthrate is plunging, it is desperately searching for immigrants, and it is encouraging childbearing among the Quebecois. The province ought to be encouraging students with French-language skills to come to Quebec. Instead of drawing other Canadians to the province's universities, Quebec encourages them to stay away. Bad for Quebec, bad for Canada.

Almost Everyone Is Eligible

There was a time, a couple of generations ago, when it was tough for the ordinary eighteen-year-old to get into university. Not so today. In fact it's quite easy—even for the academically challenged and sluggishly motivated—to find a place that will accept them, provided they aren't too picky about where they go. As long as students are flexible they will find that many universities aren't too choosy about who they let in. Even with close to half of all high school graduates going to a post-secondary institution, the country has long since passed the point where students have to fight for a spot, somewhere.

In Canada, the expansion of the university system began with the belief that every eligible and interested student deserved a chance to attend a post-secondary institution. That was a noble goal, so long as "eligible" meant "meeting a high standard." But from the 1960s onward, the definition began to be debased. By the 1970s, universities began to play the same role in society that high schools had played during the 1930s and 1940s. They became finishing schools for the masses, a place to grow, mature, and make a gentle transition to both adulthood and the rough world of work. By the start of the twenty-first century, Canada had one of the highest post-secondary participation rates and graduation rates among the leading industrialized nations.

Entrance standards, inevitably, have dropped, as universities have lowered the standards required for admission. One dramatic statistic illustrates this process, a statistic that should quell any doubt that grade inflation in high schools really exists. About fifty years ago, Ontario introduced a program to recognize "Ontario Scholars." Students who got an average of 80 per cent in their final year of high school (then Grade 13, now Grade 12) received this designation, and a grant of several hundred dollars. In the early days, 3 to 5 per cent of graduating students achieved this average—a phenomenal accomplishment, given that nine separate exams were involved and standards were high. By 2010, however, the 3 per cent had ballooned to nearly 50. It's possible of course that Ontario students are a great deal smarter (or better taught) in 2010 than they were in 1960, but it's far more likely that grade inflation has sucked much of the meaning out of high school grades.

More than half of Canadian universities appear to accept all students who meet the minimum qualifications, qualifications that have become increasingly easy to achieve. Several years back, almost all students in Saskatchewan who met the bar at the University of Saskatchewan or the University of Regina were admitted. And campuses such as Winnipeg, Brandon, St. Thomas, UNBSJ, Cape Breton University, Memorial University at Cornerbrook, Lakehead, and other places followed suit. The students did not necessarily get into the program of their choice—nursing is more selective than arts, business has more applicants than science—but they got in and then had the chance to switch majors and areas of study once they were on campus.

By the late 1990s the expansion of the Canadian university had met a primary objective: virtually all Canadian students could, if they were willing to move, find a place at a Canadian university.

Don't Mock the Social Sciences

Have you noticed that when politicians and the public criticize universities, they typically take aim at the social sciences and humanities? Commentators love to make fun of English, political science, education, and cultural studies, but they give engineering, physics, and chemistry a wide berth. Back when the Reform Party aimed its populist guns at the academy, MPs routinely rose in the House of Commons to mock federal funding of some odd-sounding humanities or social science research project. Hardly ever did they make fun of science-based projects (though on one memorable occasion, Reformers drew the nation's attention to a biology project related to the production of blackberry or blueberry jam—one

MP offered to introduce the scientist to his grandmother).

Critics steer clear of the sciences and applied sciences for a variety of reasons. First, few people understand exactly what the scientists are doing. It's easy to say—even if it's wrong—that there is no social merit in researching the emergence of gay culture on the Prairies, or deconstructing depictions of gender relations in Shakespearean plays. It's much harder to decide if a project on distributed embedded real-time systems, or research on the fundamental interactions of small molecules (such as substrates and drugs) with enzymes warrants federal funding.

The sciences and applied sciences have won the relevance contest hands down, even if that widely shared judgment is not really fair. Engineers build things, and they seem to be contributing directly to economic development. High-speed Internet technologies, solar cars, new welding systems— these all seem directly applicable to the present day. Scientists also tackle "real world" stuff—climate change, water pollution, genetic testing, the transmission of disease, the cause of memory loss, and the creation of new drugs. But the truth is, there are just as many esoteric, curiosity driven, and weird-seeming research projects in the sciences as in the social sciences and humanities. And that is precisely how it should be. Some of this work is not directly applicable to contemporary problems, but there is nothing in the social sciences and humanities that matches the search for the origins of the universe in pure public interest (no visiting humanities scholar has ever attracted the nationwide interest accorded Stephen Hawking in the summer of 2010).

There are just as many directly applicable and highly relevant social science and humanities research initiatives as there are in the sciences and applied sciences. Historians study the nature of the residential school movement and work with lawyers to resolve land claims. Political scientists try to explain the drop in voter participation and look for ways to bring more citizens to the voting booths. Economists explore the origins of the recent financial crisis and look for regulatory mechanisms to prevent a recurrence. Sociologists examine the relationship between religion and terrorism, and psychologists try to figure out how governments can stop people from smoking. Linguists find new ways to teach second languages, and cultural studies specialists look at how video games are affecting social relations and children's involvement with the education system.

It's true, many humanities and social science projects address questions internal to the disciplines and are not of immediate interest to the public at large, but a great deal of effort is being made by these researchers—just as with scientists and applied scientists—to address practical and contemporary problems.

It's too bad that the sciences and applied sciences capture the public's imagination in a way that the humanities and social sciences are rarely able to do. So try a little test. Grab a piece of paper and, on one side, write down the top five or ten things that worry you most in the world. On the other side, write down the same number of things that bring you the greatest pleasure. The answers are pretty consistent. On the worry side, the answers typically include responding to climate change, terrorism, the prospect of economic collapse, political uncertainty, religious conflict, globalization, coping with rapid technological change, and maintaining a sustainable health care system. On the positive side, people generally identify their family, their church, music, theatre, movies, love/romance, sex, literature, friends/community, shopping, recreation, and the like. Now, go back over these lists and circle all of the ones that are studied by social scientists and humanities people. Almost everything has been circled. What a powerful illustration of the importance of the social sciences and humanities!

Universities—and societies—need the sciences, applied sciences, social sciences, and humanities (and the fine and performing arts). Creating a conflict between the various university disciplines is both counterproductive and wrong. The sciences are in the ascendancy at present, largely because they (and the medical professions) have learned to play the public and politicians like a well-tuned fiddle. Social scientists and humanities specialists, perhaps because they assume what they do is self-evident, have made less effort and been less successful in alerting the public and governments to the value of their work, largely because they promote the freedom of individual faculty members and the importance of curiosity-driven research over work designed to address precise and pressing societal issues. They have a great deal to learn from their colleagues in the sciences and applied sciences.

The University Myth

The whole world is university-crazy. Only a few decades ago, universities were comparatively rare around the world and largely served the economic and social elite. Now, universities are exploding in number and diversity around the globe. There may be more than 100 million students in universities, and all but the most destitute and crisis-ridden countries are making substantial investments in university education. Countries are racing to educate their youth, all believing that a highly educated workforce is crucial to national success.

The only thing missing in this assumption is evidence. University education is a wonderful and remarkable gift. Ideally, the chance to study at university would be available to all who wish to go and have the talent and motivation to succeed. But the implicit assumption that this wonderful education will guarantee personal and national success needs to be carefully examined.

University education originally gained a high market value mainly because of its exclusivity. In times when most students did not graduate from high school, holding a university degree was a mark of real distinction. In 1961, only about 5 per cent of Canadians of all ages held university degrees. In 1971 it was about 17 per cent, and by 2006 about 23 per cent. Now, when high school graduation rates are very high, the university degree is almost ubiquitous. Similarly, countries with strong and well-functioning university systems used to have a distinct advantage over the rest of the world. The leadership in university education of the United Kingdom, Germany, and the United States in the nineteenth and twentieth centuries helped fuel national development on all social, political, economic, and cultural fronts. Countries that lagged behind—throughout Asia, the Middle East, Latin America (with exceptions such as Argentina and Brazil at times), and Africa—seemed destined to remain poor.

But the world is catching up and, in some quarters, racing ahead. China—with fewer than a million undergraduates as recently as 1997—now has more than eight million students studying at more than 2,500 public and private institutions. Even if we accept (and be careful here) the stereotype of the Chinese student as narrowly trained, uncritical, and unoriginal, the sheer size and scope of the Chinese system will produce a steadily increasing number of superb graduates. Add to this the amazing growth of university education in India—where some of the most competitive institutions in the world can be found—and many other countries, and you'll realize that the West's educational advantage is dead, or at least dying.

But are our core assumptions about a university education correct? When politicians and educational advocates speak of the great value of a university education, they are right to talk about the mind-expanding, context-providing, skills-producing aspects. But other claims are disingenuous. There is enormous demand for certain university graduates—in Canada it is generally limited to the medical professions, some branches of engineering, and a few emerging technical areas—and limited demand in most others. At the same time employers are screaming for IT technicians, specialized technical personnel, millwrights, plumbers, electricians, and other applied fields. Unemployment rates among university graduates—and the almost equally depressing underemployment rates—are creeping up in the Western world. In the developing world, where people assume there is a huge demand for highly trained people, unemployment among university graduates has also become a serious problem. A 2009 report indicated that nearly 30 per cent of China's university graduates, during a time of unprecedented economic growth, could not find work. There were more unemployed Chinese graduates in 2007—almost 1 million—than there were university students in all of Canada.

Success can be a two-edged sword. If we convince governments to expand universities—and parents to pay for their children's attendance—we produce many more universities, literally tens of millions more students around the world, and a steady decline in the status and economic value of most university degrees. The very enthusiasm for expanding the university system globally may, ironically, put a serious damper on government, parental, and eventually student enthusiasm for the investment of time and money in an advanced education.

None of this diminishes the personal and intellectual value of a properly earned university degree. But the reality certainly calls into question the legitimacy of assuming continued exponential growth in undergraduate education. There is a very good chance the world will catch on to a basic truth: the golden opportunities awaiting university graduates are not infinite.

Will Universities Lead the Innovation Economy?

Governments are taking quite a gamble. They're pouring money into university research, hoping it will lay the foundation for twenty-first century economic prosperity.

From Botswana to Japan, from Finland to Taiwan, governments and their academic partners have bought into a widely shared belief that investments in basic scientific and technological research will spark economic development and growth. Huge investments in major research facilities—university laboratories, faculty researchers, and technicians—are now commonplace. The people behind the $9 billion Large Hadron Collider started lobbying for the next piece of high-tech equipment within months of its opening. Headhunting competition for scientists, typically raided from each other's laboratories, has become an international blood sport, with China and Korea fuelling a global race for talent. The argument about the commercial value of scientific and technical research is compelling, for there are clear successes—like Silicon Valley in California, Boston, and Waterloo in Canada.

But is it true? First, academic research generally translates poorly into commercial products. Very few patents, processes, or products that emerge from university laboratories make it to market. Second, university research laboratories and classrooms are rarely the birthplaces of entrepreneurs. There are some, to be sure, but university faculty who convert their academic achievements into commercial successes are few and far between.

They are, after all, academics, pursuing research driven by curiosity and supported by peer-reviewed grants. Much the same is true of technology transfer offices, patent protection assistance, and other government- and university-supported mechanisms for producing commercial success.

Instead, there is growing belief around the world that informal contact— in coffee shops and the like—between researchers and entrepreneurs is the best means of promoting commercialization. Equally, students functioning in dynamic, cutting-edge environments are often inspired to leave the limitations of the academy to pursue their commercial ideas. Many of the key people in the dot.com revolution—Bill Gates, Steve Jobs, and others—did not find universities good environments for their work and aspirations.

Science has advanced enormously through the investments in the innovation agenda. There are more and better-funded laboratories than ever. The frontiers of science and technology are being moved back rapidly. Indeed, the movement of scientific knowledge well outstrips both the efforts at commercialization and society's capacity to understand and accept change, as the experiences of nanotechnology and biotechnology demonstrate. There is more money for graduate students and for new equipment.

But innovation may kill as many jobs as it creates. A combination of market forces and technological changes has gutted the logging industry in British Columbia in recent years, eliminating many more jobs than have been created by the expansion of high-tech sectors. Improvements in robotics have allowed companies to eliminate jobs in manufacturing, just as Computer Assisted Drawing technology has resulted in mass layoffs in drafting and related fields, and computer worksheets have transformed the need for workers in the accounting areas.

Innovation is not an automatic boon to regional and national prosperity, although companies that fail to keep abreast of technological developments can find themselves uncompetitive extremely quickly. What's more, there's no assurance that innovations will remain within the region or country that spawned them. A researcher at a particular university is not compelled to bring her product or idea to market in that area or even that nation. Most universities lay claim to some portion of the financial return from such commercial developments (though the University of Waterloo leaves complete control of the intellectual property with the creator). But returns from this source are very small. Indeed, in Canada, very little commercial development actually stays here. Most is sold at predevelopment or early-stage development to companies outside Canada. In fact, Canadian taxpayers may be paying for economic growth in other countries.

There is a huge and sad irony in the relationship between innovation and university research. There are key areas where research might well contribute substantially to the creation of innovative, creative, and expanding economies. This research would come from the social sciences and humanities—areas that have been largely left out of the explosion of innovation research. There are some great researchers working in the field, but they pale by comparison—in number and resources—with the science and technology areas. There are many unanswered questions about the creation and maintenance of innovation societies. How does creativity relate to commercialization? Which forms of education best support industrial and economic innovation? What impact do community structure, multiculturalism, and local heritage have on innovation? Which policies best support, or retard, innovation? It's odd that the non-science fields have not been more fully engaged in the study of innovation, but not totally unexpected given the way that social science and humanities research have been marginalized at most universities.

Mike Lazaridis, co-CEO of Research In Motion and one of Canada's leading supporters of academic research, described university convocations as "the best technology transfer process around." Although he spent a hundred million dollars of his own money to support basic research in theoretical physics and quantum computing, he did not think universities were innovation engines by themselves. Rather, he argued, the training of bright young people, unleashed into the world as employers and entrepreneurs, was the single greatest means of promoting commercial innovation and economic prosperity. Effective use of the classroom, to Lazaridis, is the best way of ensuring Canadian prosperity.

Universities Are Like Post Offices

In 1984, in a book called *The Great Brain Robbery*, two Canadian history professors suggested that universities were, in the late twentieth century, what post offices were in the nineteenth. At that time the post office was the only physical presence of government in the community in small towns across the country. Like post offices, universities now show that the government cares about the local citizenry and is willing to spend money to provide the region's children with the opportunity to pursue their education dreams and career ambitions.

In the late 1950s, most Canadian universities were in large cities. Only a handful—Bishop's, St. Francis Xavier, Mount Allison, and Acadia—operated in smaller communities. But by the early twenty-first century almost every community in the country with a population of more than 50,000 hosted a university or a branch campus, and many smaller centres also had a community college close at hand. Just like the post office.

Who would have thought in 1960 that fifty years later there would be universities in Sydney, North Bay, Rimouski, Kelowna, and Prince George, a University College in Thompson, a satellite law program from the University of Victoria operating in Iqaluit, and Alaskan MBA courses offered in Whitehorse?

On Vancouver Island university-level courses are offered not only in Victoria by its university and its college, but at universities and colleges in Duncan, Nanaimo, Courtenay, Qualicum, Parksville, Powell River (on the mainland), Campbell River, Port Alberni, and Port Hardy. In other words, virtually every community is served, and no one on this large island lives beyond an easy commute to the nearest campus. And in BC as a whole practically every community of any size now has a post-secondary institution either in or near it. Just like the post office.

Core Courses Won't Work

It's true, as the chapter supporting core courses shows, that the idea of requiring undergraduates to take certain courses, usually in their first year, is a seductive one for academics. Depending on your world view, you could draw up a number of lists of what you think they should take: a Marxist, for example, would come up with quite a different list than would a conservative. The other attractive idea behind the proposal is that young adults of eighteen are not fit judges of what they ought to know, and should not approach university as though it were a smorgasbord. Rather, they should learn what wiser people tell them to learn, at least for their first year. It's also hard to argue with this. In fact, the idea of core courses is a sound one; the reason that it won't work is purely practical. But universities live in an increasingly practical universe.

The idea of compulsory first-year courses has been put into practice at a number of American universities, and a few in Canada. The American ones are liberal arts colleges where all the first-year students take the same courses. At a number of places, incoming students are required to read a package of material the summer before their first enrolment, and they discuss their reading when they arrive.

It sounds good, but it won't work in this country, except in very limited circumstances. First, there are no purely liberal arts colleges in Canada, so there is almost no student body that would be sympathetic to the idea, King's in Halifax notwithstanding. The average student heading for a degree in forestry is not going to be keen on spending an entire year immersed in great ideas rather than in silviculture. This wouldn't matter if universities could compel students; but they can't. And this is the main reason why the idea of core courses won't work: our universities exist in a world where the student as consumer is dominant.

You can imagine a situation at a liberal arts college where all the students are keen on the idea of a course in Great Ideas of the Western World. Entry to the college is highly competitive; the students feel lucky to be there and have bought into the institutional philosophy. The professor is excellent, the lectures fascinating, the discussion groups enlightening. But this is Swarthmore or Grinnell, not the University of Alberta. Imagine, on the other hand, a room full of resentful business students dragooned into such a class at the U of A, sitting at the back chatting or surfing the internet on their laptops, glaring at the poor professor who got stuck with that Great Ideas class, trying to figure out how to get through the course with the least possible effort, and without ever opening their mouths in class except to talk to one another.

Two generations have gone by since the Hall-Dennis report in Ontario (1968) recommended student-centred learning, and students take their right to choose in education, as in most other things, as a matter of course. If Canadian universities were hard to get into—if we had universities that have twenty applications for each space like some of the elite American institutions—those universities could make students take what courses they liked, as the American universities do. But they aren't, and they can't. Students as consumers call the tune, and they want to choose what they study. Few universities will dare to buck this fact. UNBC abandoned its core courses. The idea won't work.

The Mandate for Universities Is Confusing

What seems so simple—universities are designed to provide high-quality teaching and research—has been complicated by changing government expectations and the demands of society. Governments have given universities contradictory and unachievable mandates. As well as teaching and conducting research, universities are now expected to:

- Promote and underpin regional economic development.
- Provide accessibility for local students.

- Offer remedial assistance for students at risk or people with significant academic deficiencies.
- Accept responsibility for responding to new social requirements. In recent years this has included providing more assistance to students with learning and physical disabilities, supporting Aboriginal students, adjusting academic programs to respond to issues of gender, sexuality, ethnicity, and the like.
- Promote the commercialization of academic research, spawning new businesses and supporting industrial growth.
- Support cultural and artistic activity.
- Encourage civic engagement and citizenship.
- Represent the community/region at the national and international level.

These and other challenges are formidable and important. Universities are funded to provide educational opportunities—and they use a good portion of the funding to foster research activity. New responsibilities, added irregularly and rarely with sufficient funding, have skewed institutional life, placed enormous pressure on university administrators, and made faculty jobs much more difficult. They have left universities with a profound sense of being overwhelmed.

Popular Culture Distorts Our Perception of University Life

Movies, television, and novels have given us a distorted notion of what university life is like. Years ago the film *Animal House* celebrated, in a perverse way, the youth culture of the modern academy, just as *The Paper Chase* dramatized the intense intellectual and professional challenges of law school. Colleges and universities are classic fare for American television and movies, producing an image of engagement, challenge, social relationships, and personal development that reinforces the North American preoccupation with attending university. (Deans, understandably, fare very poorly in the popular media, generally coming across as bumbling incompetents, ferocious taskmasters, or perverted bureaucrats.)

Occasionally they give us glimpses inside the classroom—we saw Indiana Jones on the podium briefly—but most focus on the hedonistic lifestyles of college students in the dorms, sororities, and fraternities. Slasher films and murder mysteries are fairly common. Romances, like the tearjerker *Love Story*, are standard fare. In general, the television programs and movies show kids having fun, stressing out over their studies (but leaving the homework to a small number of geeks and Math students), fighting with the establishment, and using the experience to put distance between themselves, their high school past, and their parents.

Less well known is the raunchy pornography of the distressingly successful *Girls Gone Wild* series of videos and DVDs. There is an odd Canadian twist to this phenomenon. Most of the girls—and most are claimed to be college and university students—are "discovered" in bars or parties. Since Canada has a lower drinking age than most American states, the series promoters discovered a terrific opportunity in this country to attract more of the legal-age eighteen-year-olds who were particularly popular among series subscribers.

Canadian media pay much less attention to the university experience, with one major exception. *The Decline of the American Empire*, Denys Arcand's biting and brilliant portrayal of life in a Quebec university history department, has no English-Canadian counterpart. There are glimpses of the academy in the work of a few of our novelists—notably Robertson Davies—but these are infrequent and have not penetrated the public consciousness. There is, in fact, no Canadian variant of the popular culture image-making of the United States. So, in typical Canadian fashion, we expropriate and absorb the American version, which has the effect of idealizing the American experience and making Canada's schools seem drab and uninteresting by comparison.

90   The Death of the Holistic University Experience

A long time ago, the university experience was a neat package: four years of study and fun—the hallowed halls, the kindly but dotty profs, the attractive dating and marriage prospects, first-year initiations, fraternities, sororities, beer, football, graduation—all of it. This is still the way some people think of college life, but if the university experience was ever like this, it won't be much longer.

The reality of the university system is that it's fragmenting in important ways. Students can get degrees at colleges and from on-line institutions inside and outside Canada. They often work half time or more while studying—so much for the all-in experience of being a student. Participation in campus events is down, many students still live at home, faculty are preoccupied with research and service and have less time for their students. Indeed, they appear on campus a great deal less than before, or are spending more time in their laboratories. And so many students are ill prepared, they often find themselves seeking remedial help and learning basic skills while trying to keep up with university-level content.

The traditional approach to a university education—finish high school, enroll in college, complete a degree, and then move into the workforce—has been replaced by educational anarchy. Some students take time off before coming to university. Others spend time in college and then shift. They finish university and then go to a college for practical study. They continue their work at the graduate or professional school level. They drop out, as much for financial and personal reasons as academic ones, and find work or travel. They switch majors and move between universities. In commuter schools, they often spend much of their university careers with high school friends. On campuses with large numbers of international students, students tend to socialize in separate spheres. Bonding and international exchange rarely happens—though, thankfully, romance remains alive and manages to leap cultural barriers.

New educational institutions are emerging to respond to changing realities. Some places have expanded on-line and distance learning. Private institutes are popping up, offering both on-line and face-to-face instruction. Universities have lost a big portion of the adult learner market to for-profit programs. They are no longer the only show in town on the advanced educational front. The same holds true for discovery and innovation. A great deal of research has shifted off campus, to think-tanks, private companies, government agencies, and other institutions. Journalists and freelance writers are more likely to write provocative books and articles than academics. In many ways, universities are no longer in the forefront of places that are generating the big ideas and challenges to the status quo.

The university system has changed—and we believe the shifts are both profound and permanent. The cloistered, safe, and systematic environment of the past—with students, faculty, and staff sharing in a common campus life experience that sparked life-changing learning and original research—can still be seen in places, even on the biggest campuses. But the fragmentation of the lives of students and faculty has been like a rock hitting the windshield of a speeding car. We can still see ahead, but the cracks in the university system are growing as fast as a windshield star in minus-forty-degree weather. Our collective vision of what universities are, and what they should be, is being obscured and our view of the way forward is getting very blurry. Canadians cling to the old view of what a university should be because it is familiar and comforting. But it's not a view that's consistent with the realities of the early twenty-first century.

Canada Needs More Science and Technology Graduates

There's a growing belief that global competitiveness is defined largely by university attendance and graduation rates. We think that is wrong.

University education has expanded enormously in the last fifty years, yet the greatest growth spurt is still in the offing as China, South Asia, and Africa come fully on stream. It is an article of faith that university education equals economic competitiveness—an argument that Cuba, with a remarkable level of post-secondary participation and graduation, seems to disprove. The issue is not, "Are producing enough university graduates?" but, "Are we producing enough graduates in the right fields?" It doesn't help that the definition of "right fields" shifts each decade. It makes academic nimbleness a prerequisite for ongoing economic success.

This may sound like an odd argument from a pair of historians. We believe that all students—regardless of their areas of interest—benefit enormously from the insights and abilities associated with the humanities, social sciences, and fine arts. We would like nothing more than to see all students exposed to more arts courses, just as we would like arts students to be exposed more to the science and technological fields. There are enormous advantages in having a broadly educated citizenry and in ensuring that all university graduates have a strong understanding of social, cultural, political, moral, artistic, and economic realities.

But universities have accepted—even pushed—the argument that they play an essential role in ensuring national competitiveness. Companies beg for additional graduates in the "hot" fields and pressure governments to expand opportunities. In some countries—India is the best example— places in the top schools are allocated on two criteria: the students' abilities, and national need. In Canada the top priority is student choice. Sure, there are caps on the most popular programs, but given that universities use application numbers to lobby for more funding and to determine aspects of internal allocations, these tend to be short-term.

So Canada has got roughly the university system the students want— which we think is very different from the university system the country needs. We'll end up with the world that analyst Rick Miner described as *People Without Jobs, Jobs Without People*. Colleges generally do a much better job of responding to market realities—opening, dropping, expanding, or contracting programs as the employment situation dictates. Universities change more slowly, particularly in the areas of faculty hiring and program development, which makes them much less responsive.

It's clear that the twenty-first century will be dominated by rapid innovations in science and technology, and will present many possibilities in medicine, genetics, biotechnology, nanotechnology, clean technologies, and the like. If Canadian universities are to remain competitive they will have to prepare more of the right kind of graduates. This requires a much stronger emphasis on engineering, a shift from the basic sciences to the applied sciences, and greater interdisciplinary study. The combined arts and science degrees offered at universities such as the University of New Brunswick and McMaster are already highly popular and successful. They will be classic twenty-first century degrees.

Universities will also have to adapt in two other ways. First, they'll have to work more closely with employers, both public and private, and build experience learning into more of their programs. Direct connections with the workplace will be essential if the country is to match opportunities and human resources. Second, they will have to think and plan much more quickly. New programs (many of them a year or two in length and built off basic foundational studies) will have to be developed faster—within months instead of years—and they will likely operate for a short period of time. The future will see fewer degrees like Bachelor of Science in Biology and more Bachelor of Biology (Genetic Modelling) and Bachelor of Biology (Environmental Remediation).

We can hear our colleagues in the arts screaming at us already. Not to worry: their disciplines will always have a crucial role to play in the university and society as a whole. Ironically, limiting the number of places in the arts will actually make them more competitive and likely produce stronger students and better graduates. Be brave, colleagues, and remember that what is at stake here is the economic competitiveness and viability of the country.

92 We Need a Steady Supply of International Students

Amit Chakma, President of the University of Western Ontario (now bearing the new name of Western University), chaired a national task force on international education. Its final report ended with a ringing statement: "International education in all its facets brings tremendous value to every community in Canada, whether urban or rural, eastern or western, francophone or anglophone." Canadian universities have already committed themselves to international recruitment in a big way, raising important questions about the role of international students in Canada.

In 2011, Canada attracted 240,000 international students: 60,000 from China, 24,000 from Korea, 17,000 from India, 13,000 from Saudi Arabia, 10,000 from France, and 11,000 from the United States. The number of American students studying in Canadian universities is puzzlingly low, particularly given that our schools are generally less expensive and often of higher quality than the ones back home. Perhaps the lower numbers are the result of the low-level but persistent anti-American tone they find on our campuses, particularly from some faculty members. International students spend $8 billion on tuition and other expenses, a sum that translates to 86,570 jobs and $455 million in government tax revenue. With shortages of students at some universities, particularly in the math and science disciplines, Canadian universities are committed to expanding their international recruitment efforts in the coming years.

Universities increasingly need international students to pay the bills. While they speak enthusiastically about the cultural and social benefits of having students from around the world on campus—claims that, in our experience, are overstated from the perspectives of both domestic and international students—the primary interest is financial. $8 billion is a great deal of money. As domestic recruitment becomes more challenging, international students will both fill in the student body and provide an income boost. There are costs associated with having large numbers of international students, including the costs of recruiting (agent fees, recruiting fairs, and travellers' visits), English as a Second Language training, and special on-campus services for international students. Still, universities, particularly open-access ones, rely on a steady infusion of students from overseas.

Canada, of course, does not have the international recruiting field to itself ,and the numbers of students coming to this country varies quite a bit from year to year. The number of international students attending American universities fell off and then, thanks to a more favourable exchange rate in the key Chinese market and the gold-standard brand of the American universities, rebounded. Other countries—the United Kingdom, New Zealand, various European nations and, in Asia, Malaysia, China, Japan and Korea—are fighting over the same pool of foreign students. Much of the demand comes from a small number of countries—China, India, Korea, Taiwan—which are in the process of expanding their domestic universities at a very rapid pace. In short, there are no guarantees in international recruiting.

The number of well-qualified international students interested in Canada is not infinite, and we have several disadvantages when it comes to attracting them. We are not well known internationally, and our national recruiting efforts have been uncompetitive with those of the other leading nations. Canada's weather is a further disincentive for many students. Alternatively, the possibility of turning a university degree into a permanent immigration status is a major inducement. There are problems with verifying foreign credentials, something that has caused scandals at a few American universities. Top international students—often educated in high-quality private and international high schools or the best public schools—are very attractive to leading universities. Institutions such as McGill, UBC, and Waterloo generally secure impressive candidates, many of whom likely also applied to top American, Australian, and UK schools. Lower-ranked Canadian schools, particularly in regional centres, attract a very different pool of candidates, often with lower English scores and therefore more challenges adapting to the first-year environment.

A couple of years of sharp decline have sparked a national debate about universities' reliance on international students. While these students play a crucial role in Canadian universities, it is not clear that the optimistic forecasts about their future importance will hold. Competitor nations are rolling out the big guns; they need the foreign students for the same reasons that Canadian schools are after them. Universities in their home countries, of increasingly higher quality, are ramping up to meet the demand. At the same time, graduates returning from foreign universities are encountering difficulties reintegrating into their home economies. What used to be a premium of a North American education has been eroded as the number of foreign-trained students escalates. With unemployment rates for university graduates running very high in many countries, it is also not clear that the international educational surge will continue indefinitely.

Canadian universities have gambled heavily on international students. A growing number of institutions are significantly dependent on attracting foreign applicants. If recruiting efforts falter—and this could happen if the attractiveness of Canada declines, if foreign economies (particularly China) stall, or if the pool of qualified students shrinks—some Canadian universities could be in real difficulty. They could find themselves, as did Australian universities, forced into making major changes and adjusting their offerings to meet international market needs. The current enthusiasm for international recruitment understates the significant risks and institution-changing requirements associated with attracting international students to this country.

Some of Our Best Grads Are Leaving

Where do students want to go when they graduate? When Ontario students are polled (unscientifically, we should add), most say they expect to stay in Ontario, but some say they would seriously consider relocating to the United States. At least a quarter declare an openness to head to Europe or Asia. A much smaller group—perhaps 15 per cent—are open to BC or Alberta. Ask about Saskatchewan and the Maritimes and the students roll their eyes. Ah, Ontario…

There's a worrisome message here for Canadians. A sizable number of university students are willing—some are even eager—to leave the country upon graduation. They don't seem to need huge incentives to leave: the prospect of finding a job more easily, getting a slightly higher salary, and living in a warmer place seem to be enough to get them looking beyond the borders.

It is not that Canadian university students are leaving the country in droves, like educated rats leaving a sinking ship. Most will in fact stay, many in their province of education. International students and new Canadians often return to their country of origin, a fairly logical part of the life cycle but a trend that is accelerating with the economic rise of China and India.

The problem rests not with the average graduate, but with the departure of key people, those with either entrepreneurial drive or highly specialized skills. Companies often need employees with very specific training, so the loss of these people can make it difficult for local firms to operate. These, of course, are precisely the graduates most likely to leave, to chase the greater venture-capital pots or higher-paying, exciting jobs in other places. Some of the key graduates from Canada's universities—the number and percentage remain uncertain—may be lost soon after they finish their studies.

Saskatchewan has tried to deal with the issue by instituting a Graduate Retention Program that provides a rebate of up to $20,000 for university graduates who have graduated from a provincial institution and who live and pay income taxes in the province. It has recently been expanded to include graduates from outside the province (and outside Canada) who move to the province and work there.

There's an interesting twist to this issue. When students at one large gathering were challenged as to why they were so willing to leave and—as a provocation to challenge them—so disloyal to the country that had supported them so well, they sat soberly. One student put up his hand: "Well sir, no one ever asked me to stay." So we must ask them to stay. We need the best and brightest to stay here, unless our long-term plan is either that of the Maritimes—sending the graduates "down the road"—or the Philippines, hoping that the overseas workers will send remittances back home to keep the country afloat. Neither option is good for Canada.

Struggling with English

A university degree is supposed to convey a clear indication that its holder has demonstrated proficiency in a core set of advanced skills. A Math degree indicates that the graduate has proficiency in mathematics. A French degree implies that the graduate can speak and read French at an advanced level and has a solid grounding in the cultures of the French-speaking world. And so it goes through the list of degrees.

The broader range of proficiencies is implied rather than made explicit. If you look at the recruiting materials from universities, the list is fairly clear: critical thinking, research capabilities, analytical abilities, and presentation skills. The most fundamental promise, however, of an English language institution is the ability to speak and write English. It is not at all clear that this most fundamental requirement is being met.

A highly successful Chinese-Canadian entrepreneur who works in various areas of Canada-China trade and investment told us that, over the years, she has hired many university graduates to work in her companies, looking in particular for people who can communicate in both Chinese and English. To her constant dismay, most of the graduates she has hired have had serious deficiencies with English. While they could, as a group, speak English at a professional level, their writing abilities were such that they could not be relied on to write properly in English. She recognized that the problem rested with the difficulty of making the transition from speaking and writing Mandarin or Cantonese to working at a high level in English. But she was also dismayed that an undergraduate degree from a highly ranked Canadian university was not a guarantee of English language ability. More alarmingly, the same is true of too many native-born Canadians.

There is no simple explanation for the problems with English among Canadian-born university graduates, although a strong possibility is the abandonment of rigorous standards for high school graduation. Standards of academic writing across the Canadian primary and secondary education systems clearly require attention, for students who are not well-trained in high school will have difficulty catching up at the university level. While there is a tendency to see the English language issues as being a function of increased international student recruitment, that is only part of the challenge. A sizeable number of Canadian students were either foreign born and have English as a second language or were raised in households where English was the second language. These students often have advanced proficiency in another language, or more than one; they are often very literate—just not in English.

International students, of course, face particular challenges. They have had to study English—often in high schools overseas—and have to pass an ESL proficiency test to get into Canadian universities. Many take a transitional English course before they start their classes. Completing such a course is often a requirement of admission for students who fail to secure a high enough grade on their ESL test. Many of these students, uncertain in their use of English, enrol in science and math-based programs that require minimal English skills. In general, however, the ESL entrance requirements are not really an assurance of academic success in English-rich courses and programs. With many of the students spending a lot of time with people from their own country, often living together off campus, the opportunities for casual use of English are limited. Many international students, often very talented in other areas, fail to develop beyond the most basic English skills.

It really misses the point to focus on international and foreign-born students. Many students come to university with weak English writing skills and many will graduate without making a significant improvement. There are many reasons for this. Large first-year classes, a wide-spread reliance on multiple-choice examinations, limited opportunities to practise writing, minimal feedback from instructors, and few support services contribute to an English-deficient academic environment. With many professors lacking the time to pay close attention to students' writing abilities or believing that advanced English skills are someone else's responsibility, there is no campus-wide commitment to improving English proficiency. The harsh truth is that there are a fair number of university courses and programs that do not require much proficiency in English and since, in many institutions, introductory English courses are either easy or non-compulsory, students can graduate without a strong language skill.

When Australia conducted a national survey of the English language ability of international students, the results shocked the nation. Over one third of the graduates were not fully literate in English. No such survey has been completed in Canada, which means that the Canadian public does not know the dimensions of the problem.

A university degree must, if it is to be credible, contain a guarantee that the graduate has a high level of achievement in areas of basic competency. At present, Canadian universities cannot say with confidence that their graduates have high-level English language writing abilities. They should be tackling this issue as a matter of urgency, lest the stature of the Canadian degree erode further.

Digital Technologies

A decade or so ago, when Conrad Black was in his ascendancy, newspapers and local radio stations were seen as a licence to print money, and the music industry seemed to have a hammerlock on kids' wallets. Then the digital revolution hit. Napster made copying music a snap. BitTorrent introduced file sharing to youth culture and transformed movie viewing from an evening at the theatre to a cozy snuggle with one's laptop. On-line newspapers, radio stations, blogs, discussion forums, and the like nibbled away at the information lifeblood of the news industry, and Kijiji and craigslist drove a stake through the want-ads, the heart of the newspapers' business models. What a change—and in such a short time.

Many people think that universities will be on the hit list soon. University education, particularly as practiced in Canada, is very old tech and very low tech. Classrooms might have projection capabilities and professors might put their notes online, but Canadian universities are only playing on the fringes of the digital revolution.

The warning signs are out there—the new technologies are transforming the way students learn and the way universities teach. In many countries, huge online universities, with 200,000 students or more, provide education to students through digital means.

What do the following institutions have in common: Alama Iqbal Open University (Pakistan), Indira Gandhi National Open University (India), Anadolu University (Turkey), Universitas Terbuka (Indonesia), Bangladesh Open University (Bangladesh)? First, they are all distance education/online universities (Anadolu has a traditional campus but the online section is by far the largest, enrolling more than 870,000 students). Second, they are all in the top ten largest universities in the world—Alama Iqbal has three million students; Bangladesh Open University has a mere 600,000 and is seventh largest.

Some North American public institutions are adapting to the new technologies. The Western Governors University, an online consortium of American schools, has more than 19,000 students. The largest digital university in the United States, the University of Phoenix Online, has more than 220,000 students (or more than the University of Toronto, Alberta, British Columbia, and the University of Montreal combined) the largest conventional university in the States, Ohio State, has a mere 53,000 students (or fewer than the University of Toronto).

The biggest Canadian competitors—Athabasca University (38,000 students, most studying by distance education), the Open University of British Columbia/Thompson Rivers University, and Télé-université Québec—are much smaller and serve targeted audiences. The Ontario government announced in 2010 a significant shift towards distance education/online learning, although it hasn't unveiled a formal plan yet.

Online education, however, may only be the tip of the iceberg. Students' use of technology—from iPhones to BlackBerrys, instant messaging to Google—is well ahead of most instructors'. So too have their learning styles, attention spans, and understanding of expertise and knowledge been transformed by instant access to the Internet. Interactions with peers, now encouraged through seminars and discussion groups, will take place globally by video-conferencing devices, likely working through portable devices or home computers. Academic research—both the collection of data and the sharing of results and ideas—has yet to catch up with the possibilities of the new technologies—let alone the technologies coming down the line. The role of professors will likely change dramatically, as will learning styles.

In a decade or so, massive investments in physical classrooms, long-term commitments to tenure-stream faculty, and even the concept of the old-style residential campus could well seem archaic, or at best a luxury for the rich.

And further down the line, who knows? University degrees by intravenous injection? What we do know is that major change is in the offing, student expectations are shifting dramatically, and great opportunities await the institutions and jurisdictions that first figure out the new way forward. Ironically, although university researchers played such a big role in the development of the Internet and new digital devices, universities appear to be well behind the curve in making the most of the digital age.

Lower-Income Families and Universities

A central promise of the Canadian university system is accessibility. It's the main thing most politicians talk about when they mention universities: space for voters' kids. For fifty years, governments across the country have tried to ensure that any qualified Canadian could attend university and, by and large, they have been successful. Students from a wide variety of socioeconomic, cultural, and ethnic backgrounds have made their way into our universities. In an age when Canada has been committed to equality of opportunity and equality of circumstances, opening universities to young people from all backgrounds has been a major national accomplishment. Getting previously underrepresented groups into our universities has been a success. Women now outnumber men on campus. New Canadians, particularly those from East and South Asia, have arrived in large numbers and have come to dominate certain science and technology fields. More

Aboriginal students and students from small towns and rural areas have come to university. Overall, the great Canadian accessibility campaign has worked, insofar as it has put many students from diverse backgrounds into first-year classes.

But there is a warning sign flashing over the Canadian system: Canadians from working-class and poor backgrounds are still much less likely to attend university than are those from wealthier, middle-class backgrounds. Slightly more than one-half (50.2 per cent) of youth from families in the top quartile of the income distribution attend university by age nineteen, compared to less than a third of youth from families in the bottom quartile (31.0 per cent). Those Canadians for whom a publicly supported university degree is meant to provide the much-needed leg up into the middle class are not taking advantage of the opportunity in the anticipated numbers.

Research suggests several reasons for this. First, students and their parents over-estimate the cost of attending university—in large measure, one suspects, because of all the public talk about high tuition, mounting student debt, and the need to set aside close to $15,000 per year for an undergraduate education. Second, these same families may well be skeptical, and with good reason, about the benefits of a university degree. Putting these two together—exaggerate the costs and underestimate the returns—makes a university education look like a bad deal. Not surprisingly, then, many of them opt not to attend university. Research also shows, not surprisingly, that poor kids can do worse in school and on standardized tests, for reasons which have nothing to do with their intelligence.

Of course, lower-income students often have very little or no financial backing. If they run into financial difficulty, they might have to leave the university. If they graduate with a sizeable debt and do not find a decent job, they could again find themselves in serious financial difficulty. More well-to-do Canadians have parental or family back-up of one form or another, should they become overstretched. Universities have bursaries and scholarships and most have emergency assistance for students in severe financial difficulty, but students sometimes do not understand that support is available or do not understand how to get access to the funds.

Given both what has been happening in the Canadian job market for university graduates and the effects of rising student debt on the current generation of young adults, it appears that the calculations of lower-income Canadians make a good deal of sense. The costs of university are high and getting higher. The financial returns for many university graduates can be much lower than expected. With unemployment and underemployment rates very high, economic prospects are more mixed than has long been believed. While universities and governments are concerned about the decline in enrolment among poor and working-class Canadians, it is possible that the young adults and their families are wise to be cautious about their educational and career choices. As for helping them financially, the money might be better spent at an earlier stage of their education, before bad circumstances make university impossible for them.

97 Do Our Business Schools Have a Future?

For the past thirty years, business schools have been on a roll. From modest beginnings in the 1970s, they have grown in status, size, stature, and public importance. There are, rather surprisingly, sixty-three of them across Canada. The Canadian Association of Business Students claims to represent 75,000 students at twenty-seven of these schools. Business schools have secured multi-million-dollar donations, which is why many of them are now named after philanthropists—and pay handsome salaries to their professors. The top business schools charge a great deal for their undergraduate programs, with the School of Accounting and Finance at the University of Waterloo charging $18,000 a year. MBA programs are even more expensive—the one-year Executive MBA program at the University of Toronto's Rotman School of Business costs $96,000 as of 2013 and the one at Queen's costs almost as much. This may seem like a lot of money, but the program's website claims that graduates of Queen's Executive MBA

(25 per cent of the fees for which are recoverable as a tax deduction) will recoup their cost in three to four years of enhanced salary. Business schools are big-money affairs.

The business schools attract excellent students. Parents are generally supportive of business education, and see it as a sensible, career-oriented degree. The best schools are extremely selective, with some institutions attracting as many as ten applicants for every position in the first-year class. Companies, which increasingly seek to hire on the basis of specialized expertise, are attracted to students who have taken a practical approach to their university studies. One rental car company, for example, seeks to hire only business graduates for their rental clerk positions, holding out the prospect of rapid promotion within the company for successful new employees.

Faculty salaries at the leading schools are routinely above $200,000 and some specialists command half again as much. The major donations help, with many schools receiving contributions of $10 to $15 million in return for naming rights. But even these seemingly large sums make a relatively small dent in the annual budget. (The return on a $10 million donation is approximately $400,000 a year, or about enough for two professors' salaries.) Student demand has allowed business schools to raise their fees, but a fair bit of the money is committed to impressive new buildings and attractive facilities. Business schools have learned, not surprisingly, that students who pay a lot of money for a service demand a high-quality product.

The private sector supports business schools strongly, often to the detriment of the rest of the campus. Many focus their internships and co-op placements on the business schools, recruit heavily among the graduating class, contribute financially to the business school, hire faculty as consultants, and sponsor business school events. In many ways, business schools have become quasi-independent, marching to a different drummer and less beholden to the central administration than are most other units. Queen's Business School contemplated separation from the campus some time back and came close to pulling it off, settling for sovereignty association instead.

Will the run last? It's hard to say. Roger Martin, the dean of the Rotman School, completed a study of the economic value of an undergraduate business degree. He concluded that the overproduction of degree holders has removed the market premium for graduates. There is market demand for graduates in selected business programs, including finance, high-end MBAs and accounting, but much less for the now generic basic business degree. The rest of the campus is often jealous of the achievements of business schools—particularly high faculty salaries, extensive student supports, and attractive buildings. The business school operations distort campus life and lead to the creation of special salary categories and financial arrangements for the colleges—much to the dismay of colleagues at the university. There have also been high-profile controversies, at York and Carleton in particular, over big donations by businessmen (though in these cases not to business schools) where it was perceived by some faculty that the donors were seeking too much control over the operations of the centres that they were funding.

It is likely that the proliferation of MBA and other such programs will eventually diminish the value of the degree, if it has not done so already. Producing so many graduates will, in turn, likely create oversupply and the subsequent problem of underemployment.

But there is another problem that needs to be raised: Canadian productivity, innovation, and entrepreneurship all lag behind international competitors. The rhetoric behind the expansion of Canadian business schools has focused on the need for Canada to produce the specialists, particularly the entrepreneurs, who would lead the country toward greater international competitiveness. Instead, in a twenty-year period of steady growth in Canadian business school enrolment, business-related research, and faculty engagement with the business community, Canada's key indicators of productivity and innovation have plummeted in comparison to the United States'. This is not to suggest that the business schools are responsible for the decline; the challenge rests more with the investment patterns and conservatism of Canadian business. But it does suggest that the business schools are not likely to be the solution. If Canadian universities are to lead the country to greater competitiveness, they will need a different approach than a continued investment in business schools.

98 Is There a Student Debt Crisis?

University costs a lot of money; though, as we argued earlier, in many cases it is money well spent. Tuition fees, except in Quebec, are in the $5,000 to $6,000 range for a basic Arts or Science degree. Living costs might run between $8,000 and $10,000 a year. Books and supplies can easily add another $1,000. Collectively, this adds up to around $17,000 a year or close to $70,000 per four-year degree for students who manage to finish their degrees in four years. Even with a Registered Education Savings Plan, parental support, and/or part-time work and a summer job, many students find that they need other funds to cover their costs. The money can come from the Canadian Student Loans program, administered by provincial authorities, from family members, or from private loans.

Student debt has emerged as a major burden. Students graduating into what is for many an uncertain and low-wage job market can find themselves with substantial debts. The average debt load of the students who have debt (about half don't) is $28,000. It can take years for some graduates to pay back their loans, a situation that can interfere with plans to get married, start a family, buy a house, or otherwise get on with life. The problems are particularly acute for students from low-income families, where parental and other support is often not available. The student debt crisis, which is at critical levels in the United States and which is emerging as a major problem in Canada, raises basic questions about the way a university education is financed.

Not all student debt is a serious burden. If a student has a four-year degree in a high-demand area, with good job prospects, a $10,000 to $20,000 debt is hardly a crisis. Conversely, a graduate student with $40,000 or more in debt who holds a degree in a subject for which there is not much demand may be in serious financial trouble. The graduating class, then, can be divided into various groupings: no debt, low debt, significant debt but strong earning potential, significant debt but limited earning potential, and very high debt. The first three groups are not at serious risk; the last two are.

You might argue that some of this debt is avoidable. A student might live with her parents in Hamilton and go to McMaster, or she may decide that she's had enough of them and attend York, living in Toronto on borrowed money. If a student opts to live on his own rather than staying in residence, incurring additional costs as a result, are these extra expenses that the public should be worried about? If he takes out substantial student loans and uses part of the money to pay for lifestyle costs such as a car, a skiing vacation, or other non-essentials, should this be a matter of government concern? It is impossible to know how students spend their money, of course, and really none of anyone's business, unless they want the taxpayer to supply it. The vast majority use their money responsibly and budget carefully; the irresponsible few, as is always the case, can undermine public support for the rest of the students.

The basic problem rests not with debt but with the relationship between debt and work. We know that many students have unrealistic expectations about jobs, careers, and earnings. It is inevitable that students who anticipate high incomes and solid career prospects will incur more debt in the expectation that they can easily repay the loans shortly after they start work. If the vast majority of university graduates were able to find a decent job shortly after leaving university, there would be no student debt crisis. Even a $40,000 student debt to a young adult with a $60,000 a year job and decent prospects is not insurmountable. A $20,000 debt for a young person earning $30,000 a year (or, worse still, who is jobless) is a problem, and potentially a serious crisis. In the current economic circumstances, with jobs in short supply and with a disconnect between university degrees and the employment market, it is inevitable that a debt crisis will emerge and, potentially, become a truly serious problem for the current generation.

The fact that many students find themselves seriously in debt speaks to the importance of good financial planning before attending university. Four years of undergraduate studies are expensive, with not a large number of opportunities to make extra money. With high-paying summer jobs in short supply, many students resort to part-time work during the academic year in order to cover costs. This, in turn, limits study time, often slowing progress toward a degree. Thus the debt merry-go-round turns. Students and families need to speak frankly about the costs of attending university, and the costs and benefits of the degree program they are considering (some degrees are more worth going into debt for than others). If they do not, and if they get themselves into the world of debt, they can find themselves spending a fair part of their young adult lives paying for their degree.

Top Priority: Teaching and Learning

What would you think of a university obsessed with a single goal: being the best institution in Canada in terms of student success and satisfaction? How would you react if you knew that this mid-sized university (13,500 students) has 20,000 applications per year for 5,000 spaces for incoming students? If you were then told that this university had one of the best student/faculty ratios in the country, and was rated very high by its students for the quality of the teaching, access to faculty, and overall student satisfaction, wouldn't you be impressed?

Traditionally, universities have been change-resistant, faculty-centric, and preoccupied with research and graduate studies rather than student needs. But there are changes in the wind—as is evident by the creation of Mount Royal University in Calgary. Never heard of it? You will. This upstart institution represents a vital trend in the Canadian university system: the re-emergence of the teaching-focused, high-quality undergraduate institution.

MRU's mission statement is clear, and it doesn't talk about excellence in research: "We are an undergraduate university focused on teaching and learning informed by scholarship. We are committed to personalized, experiential, and outcome-based learning. We deliver high quality programs built on a foundation of General Education." Mount Royal has no graduate programs. Instead, it offers a wide variety of academic and career programs, almost all of which offer an experiential or work component. The university is awash with business, industry, and community advisory committees—all devoted to ensuring that graduates are career-ready. Faculty members on the teacher, scholarship, and service stream devote 60 per cent (six courses per year) of their time to teaching (as opposed to than the 40 per cent that is the Canadian standard). Those hired on the teaching and service stream teach eight courses per year. Financial and status awards highlight teaching above all else. As recently-retired Provost and Vice-President, Academic Robin Fisher said, "If you are a great researcher, you will still not get to be a Full Professor unless you are also a great teacher."

Mount Royal started as a college, overshadowed by the research-intensive University of Calgary, and was little known outside of Cowtown. It became a university in 2009. Under President David Marshall, MRU fought against an intransigent provincial government and the equally resistant provincial post-secondary system, not only for university status but also for full per-student funding as a university. Providing top-quality undergraduate teaching and student support, he argued, was as expensive as supporting research and graduate programming. Marshall insisted that Mount Royal focus its efforts on teaching and not on a divided research and teaching mandate, unlike most of the country's good small undergraduate schools (including Acadia, Bishop's, Trent, and St. Francis Xavier), which have swallowed the expensive research and graduate studies pill.

MRU is not an elite undergraduate institution like the very best American schools (Middlebury, Swarthmore, Gettysburg, Reed, or Lewis and Clark). The average class size is over twenty-six students—but 99 per cent of all classes have fifty or fewer students, so there are none of the massive first-year courses that dominate the Canadian undergraduate landscape. The graduate employment rate of 97.8 per cent (for the class of 2009/10) is no doubt helped immensely by the vibrant economy in Calgary, the city that provides almost 80 per cent of all of the students at the university. This is not a magnet school, drawing eager undergraduates from across the country. To this point, it is largely Calgary's secret.

Mount Royal is not alone in responding differently to the challenges of twenty-first century undergraduate education. The university colleges in British Columbia that were repositioned as universities—Fraser Valley, Vancouver Island, Kwantlen, Capilano, Emily Carr, Thompson Rivers—also have a strong emphasis on undergraduate teaching. MacEwan University, formerly Grant MacEwan College, in Edmonton, made the same transition as MRU, also in 2009; like MRU, it has a strong career and professional emphasis in its undergraduate programming and has made an extensive effort to ensure that its academic offerings align with graduate opportunities in research-intensive universities. MRU has been aided, in no small measure, by the massive shortage of university spaces in Calgary and Alberta generally, which has driven up demand and improved the quality of the student body (although MRU, true to its roots as a community college, has provision for alternate entry for students without stellar academic track records.)

Ontario, currently contemplating the addition of three universities to an already overcrowded undergraduate market, would do well to consider the Mount Royal model. *Academic Reform,* a provocative and important book by Ian Clark, David Trick, and Richard Van Loon, makes a convincing financial and educational case for Ontario's pursuing teaching-only under-graduate universities. The MRU example illustrates not just the institutional viability of this option, but also the many positive benefits for students, undergraduates, and communities from a properly designed and executed undergraduate university. Mount Royal University does not answer all of the challenges of undergraduate education in Canada but, with its col-league institutions in Alberta and British Columbia, it is a vital and large step in the right direction.

Our Universities: A Global Success Story

Canadians are great self-critics; we're much better at pointing out shortcom-ings and failures than at celebrating success. The authors of this book worry that we have fallen into this trap, for we have vigorously drawn attention to the problems of Canada's university system. In the end, however, it is important to step back and contemplate the relative standing of Canada's leading post-secondary institutions. The results might surprise you.

There are perhaps 10,000 universities and degree-granting colleges in the world, the number depending on which statistic you believe. The United States, the global centre of post-secondary education, has nearly 3,000, including its junior colleges! Canada has ninety-two members of the Association of Universities and Colleges of Canada, a list that includes all but a handful of small private institutions and satellite campuses of American universities. The world's universities range from tiny church-based institutions to huge distance education universities that have hundreds of thousands of students (the for-profit University of Phoenix had 600,000 in 2010 but, as of 2012, was closing some of its facilities). They include research supercentres like Harvard, with its $35 billion endowment, and ultra-expensive private institutions aimed at Brazilian and Argentinian elites. It is a strange, diverse, and complex global university system.

Within this institutional tapestry, Canada stands near the top. Twenty-two Canadian universities are ranked in the top five hundred in the world, with Toronto at twenty-seventh, UBC at thirty-ninth, and McGill at sixty-third. Our best universities—Toronto, Alberta, UBC, Waterloo—do not really match up to the major private research universities in the USA, but the average Canadian institution is better than the average American university and college. We have a university system that is of higher standard overall than those of such wealthy countries as Japan, France, and even the United Kingdom. Australia, on the other hand, with a population two-thirds of ours, does better than Canada, with nineteen universities on the list.

Canada's elite universities offer solid undergraduate programs, globally competitive graduate programs in selected fields, and fine professional programs. Several of Canada's medical schools, led by the remarkable network of medical sciences at the University of Toronto and McGill, are among the most important in the world. There are specific programs and faculties—Math at Waterloo, Oceanography at Dalhousie, Bioresources at Saskatchewan, energy research at Calgary and Alberta, Asian Studies at UBC—across the country that are truly impressive. We do not, however, have elite small liberal arts universities, mostly because of the absence of the major endowments and $50,000 a year tuition fees that make their American counterparts—Swarthmore, Grinnell, and the rest—the global standard.

Over the last decade, the world's universities have been drawn into a highly competitive and controversial ranking system—think of the *Maclean's* annual rankings done on a global scale. There are various methods of ranking, some focused on research and others weighted toward a broader set of metrics. By any of these standards, Canadians should be proud of what our universities have achieved.

Academic Ranking of World Universities (ARWU) by Shanghai Jiao Tong University, endorsed by *Maclean's* magazine

27.	University of Toronto
39.	University of British Columbia
63.	McGill University
92.	McMaster University
101–150.	University of Alberta, University of Montreal
151–200.	University of Waterloo
201–300.	Dalhousie University, Laval University, Queen's University, Simon Fraser University, The University of Calgary, Western University, University of Guelph, University of Manitoba, University of Ottawa, University of Saskatchewan
301–400.	University of Victoria
401–500.	Carleton University, University of Quebec, University of Sherbrooke, York University

That Canada has twenty-three universities in the top five hundred is truly impressive. On a per capita basis, that is much higher than the USA or Japan, though less than Australia. Japan, with four times as many people as Canada, has only twenty-five universities in the top five hundred. Any other country would see this as a major accomplishment and would applaud the commitments by federal and provincial governments that underpin this achievement. But we do not do that sort of thing in Canada.

Canadian universities have traditionally been all much the same in quality (or have been claimed to be), but that has been changing over the past decades. With emphasis on research and graduate studies, the top fifteen universities are increasingly pulling away from the pack. This means that the medium-sized and smaller universities have, over time, been losing their relative share of resources, diminishing their capacity to support regional development and to compete with the larger schools for donors, faculty members, and top students. While the range in quality is nowhere near as great as in the USA, the diversification is starting to show up in the increasing stratification of Canadian universities.

What makes the overall accomplishment of Canadian universities in research and service to students even better is they have achieved their rankings with fewer resources than most other countries. This, in turn, is a testament to the commitment and professionalism of academic administrators and faculty members. By almost any measure, Canada is well served by its universities.

Epilogue: Twenty-One Recommendations for the Future

What should universities do to prepare for the future? How can they best ensure that they will be winners and not losers in 2060? The problems are serious, and not all institutions are going to survive the next fifty years. The university and college system in Canada faces unprecedented pressures in many areas: student numbers, government funding, rising costs, public and parental expectations, contribution to economic development, and, particularly, accessibility and the capacity to address national and regional social concerns. There will never be enough money to meet these demands and expectations. The system we have, with institutionalized and professional rigidity, broken cost and funding models, and confused expectations, will have tremendous difficulty responding to the new realities. This does not mean that there is nothing that can be done (although it does suggest that universities will respond slowly—and perhaps put themselves and the system at risk by so doing). In fact, there are many important things that can and must be done to anticipate and respond to changing conditions. So, boldly sticking our necks out into the unknown, and charging recklessly into forecasting and aggressive planning, we offer the following recommendations for Canadian universities:

High quality is the number-one assurance of success. Top-quality institutions, faculties, departments and faculty members flourish. Mediocrity—which is in danger of becoming Canada's national mantra—is a death sentence. Even approaching something like the cultivation of at-risk students, typically a sign of commitment to low standards, can be tackled with a commitment to high-level achievement. In the coming years, institutions that stick to low standards will become like high schools; institutions that commit themselves to pre-eminence in some or all fields will flourish.

Be future makers, not future takers. Passivity in the face of change is a death sentence. Creative and positive response, knowing that there will be failures and stumbles along the way, is essential. Universities should establish an Institutional Future Committee, charged with monitoring social, economic, political, and cultural affairs on a national and global basis and proposing detailed responses to the university community. This committee should be one of the most prominent on campus. Universities are research institutions. They should—and do—understand the contextual forces shaping our world better than anyone. This ability has to be harnessed—and attended to—by the institutions themselves.

Specialization works. Canada, we have already argued, has more than fifty universities but really only one model for how universities operate, despite the fact that there have always been possibilities for differentiation. Ryerson Polytech could have become a degree-granting technical institution; it chose to become a university much like all of the others. There are a few mild exceptions. The oddly named University of Ontario Institute of Technology aspires to be different, but has evolved slowly. The University of Northern British Columbia carved out specific niches for itself and has flourished well beyond expectations; yet, despite its original claim to be different from older universities, it has increasingly become more and more like them. We need the courage to be different in this country, to avoid replicating the University of Toronto or McGill on a regional or local basis. One of the greatest innovations in post-secondary education in this country—still bearing fruit half a century later—was the University of Waterloo's radical decision to tie its future to co-operative education. We have had precious few substantial innovations since; instead, we have had migration toward sameness. Universities need to decide what they do best and what they do differently. And they need to allow this difference to permeate the institution. This takes courage and determination—and a willingness to be different.

Universities need to understand the differences in the student population. We have argued that students generally fit into one of three streams (with important movements between them). They are either at university for remedial assistance, for career preparation, or for academic and professional development. Universities need either to decide where their focus will be, or to develop programs that meet the needs of two or all three groups, or do both. Toronto, McGill and UBC should focus on elite students; Brandon, Cape Breton, and Corner Brook will probably do best with a mix of career preparation and remedial programming. Each institution should determine its priorities and preferred approaches. The system should stop, however, assuming that one set of programs and courses will adequately meet the needs of all students. A very small number of universities should turn themselves into elite liberal arts and sciences institutions, along the American model.

We have a two-tier faculty system, and it is time to admit it. In many countries, university faculty fit into either a research-intensive stream/institution or a teaching stream/institution. Canadian egalitarianism and an unwillingness to call a spade a spade have compelled us to pretend that everyone is both a researcher and a teacher. We now, in addition, have a vast army of contract, sessional, and part-time faculty members. These people, as the bitter York University strike of 2009 attests and as future such conflicts will re-enforce, desperately want stability, recognition, and a chance at a full career. Universities should recognize the current realities and the inevitability of the system's becoming more reliant on non-research faculty members. It is important that this change be recognized in a manner that is supportive, appropriate, and sustainable. Do away with the research requirement for these faculty members without designating them as second-class. In return, require them to teach more. The creation of two-tier faculty arrangements—essentially continuing lecturer positions for teaching-intensive faculty members and research and teaching tenure track positions—will recognize the reality of the contemporary environment and provide protection and security for a cadre of excellent and deserving university teachers, while acknowledging the real needs of the university environment.

Career Readiness should be a key policy of the modern university system. Faculty members like to argue—correctly—that universities were not created to provide career training. Universities were, and are, for the education of the citizenry. But universities have not been able to convince government, parents, employers, or even students of this—and this horse has long since fled the barn. People expect universities to produce career-ready graduates—and the students themselves are at the forefront of this demand. Universities can maintain many of their programs and courses as at present, but they need to expand career preparation programs for undergraduates, add professional master's programs for graduates, develop new and more intense ties with employers, and adjust some of what they do to ensure that graduates are, indeed, heading into the workforce fully prepared and ready for exciting and dynamic careers.

Colleges and universities need to integrate their offerings in creative and mutually beneficial ways. At present, colleges and universities look at each other with suspicion and mild contempt. Colleges are practical; universities are theoretical. Colleges provide open access; universities are elitist. Colleges are for doers, universities for thinkers. These distinctions do no one any good; it is high time that the institutions began to co-operate. Some colleges and universities have done so, to the betterment of both. Co-ordinated offerings—including arrangements where students enrol in both college and university at the same time and, perhaps, complete both a college diploma and a university degree in a five-year period—should become commonplace. The academically elite institutions are, however, unlikely to go far down this path. The locally focused institutions should take a close look at models like Nipissing University and Canadore College, two institutions that share a common footprint in North Bay.

Tenure has to go—or at least it has to change. Universities have had a free ride on the institutional flexibility front, hiding behind the mystique and untouchability of tenure for professors. The reality is that major changes are needed. Academic freedom—the right to say unpopular things—must be protected from internal and external forces. Indeed, the *Charter of Rights and Freedoms* provides much of the intellectual and legal protection that tenure was originally designed to cover. (And few people know that, despite tenure, university professors are among the most active complainants to Human Rights Commissions—it seems that even tenure and its many protections and processes are not quite enough.) Academic freedom must be ensured, and indeed, university faculty should be speaking out much more

244

than they currently do. But academic freedom and job security are two very different considerations, and they must be separated. Universities must have the ability to reassign resources and faculty positions to areas of need and away from areas of declining demand. Without such a change—easily the hardest thing to do in a university setting—some universities will make General Motors look like a fast-moving start-up company in a decade or two.

Universities have to move quickly into the digital age—and they can start by requiring all students and faculty to participate in online courses. No one really knows what the digital academic future will look like, but it will be radically different on many fronts. At present, engagement with online learning (either through full courses or mixed-modal approaches) is voluntary and, at best, episodic. Universities should require all students to take a minimum of one course per semester online (there will be no magical cost saving here, but demand for lecture room space will decline significantly). They should likewise require that all faculty put one or more courses online. This is no longer an optional exercise, but rather an integral part of how people study, learn, teach, and communicate. More to the point, online learning will evolve rapidly along with new technologies; universities have to have their finger in the clay to be an effective part of designing the educational future.

Student choice in first- and second-year course offerings should be scaled back. Sorry to sound paleolithic, but universities know what students need to learn better than the students do. It is vital that all students be given more direction, rather as they are in Engineering and some science and professional programs. Getting agreement will be difficult, but if university faculty cannot define what a foundation year or two should be, then there is something wrong with their approach to education.

Competency-based learning is essential. University professors love to tell of students who come into their classes without basic writing, reading, and communication skills—and who then pass other peoples' courses without strain. Universities need to define, program by program, what skills are required of graduates. These skills should then be tied to specified mandatory courses. And students who do not develop appropriate skills in all compulsory areas should not progress or graduate. It is just as important that an Arts graduate be numerate as it is that an Engineering graduate be able to write. High-level English or French language skills must be an absolute requirement of all graduates. A university degree has to mean something clear and irrefutable. It used to, but currently it does not.

The approach to the education of international students has to change dramatically. International students can enrich campus life. Canadian universities can make and have been making significant contributions to personal development and to the betterment of those students' home countries. But in some ways they are being shortchanged by our system. English-language issues, in particular, persist. Students from other countries need to be provided with what they are seeking—a high-quality education in an English-speaking environment. Universities need to shift away from an emphasis on entrance standards to a combination of academic potential and exit standards. Most international students need degree-long assistance with English as a second language. New approaches and an emphasis on exit standards could result in major improvements in the educational experience for foreign students.

Universities need to lead the digital revolution. University students are at the cutting edge of communication innovation; their institutions languish far in the background. The pursuit of the paperless institution is still a running joke. Most university classrooms are laughable as high-technology settings. Universities in this country, working collaboratively with government and the private sector, should be at the forefront of the digital revolution. Libraries have done a superb job of putting materials on line, but student and faculty receptiveness needs to be greatly improved. Bookstores are seriously out of date in this regard but could be at the vanguard of bringing e-books into this country. E-seminars could be effectively integrated into the undergraduate and graduate experience, just as e-lectures could expand the reach and impact of faculty experience. The future of digital media likely rests with ubiquitous computing. University environments are almost ideal testing grounds for this kind of revolutionary technology. University researchers provide a great deal of the digital innovation that is changing the world; oddly, universities are very slow adopters. This has to change.

Universities need more revenue streams. At present, universities have a very small number of revenue streams. There are the big three—government grants, university tuition fees, and donations—but they are proving inadequate. Universities vary a great deal in their effectiveness at developing alternate streams. There are, for example, loyalty programs for alumni; positive returns from parking, bookstores, and residences; public-private partnerships; and other such activities. Most produce limited income. Governments and institutions placed great hope in commercialization initiatives—patents, start-up companies, licensing, and the like—but the returns there have been very disappointing. It is time to consider radical alternatives. Why do not universities buy a gas station and promote its use to students, faculty, staff, alumni, and community supporters? Some universities—Queen's, Western, Alberta, UBC—could capitalize on their brand recognition and do, as the big American universities do, earn income off residuals—how many sweatshirts does one have to sell to pay a faculty member's salary? (The answer is probably something like 100,000, so perhaps this is a bad idea.) Some universities own land and develop commercial housing. One, Guelph, runs a commercial gravel pit. Others lease out residence space for conferences. Very few have commercial consulting practices that capitalize on faculty skills (and the abilities of academic spouses, one of the greatest untapped sources of expertise in the country). Something along these lines needs to be done. Government grants will likely continue to decline. Resistance to tuition increases will continue. Donations will remain targeted at special projects and often carry additional costs to the universities. All costs will rise. Without additional revenue streams, universities will likely find themselves in a steadily accelerating fiscal nightmare in the years to come.

Universities need to rediscovery their universality. Universities used to pride themselves on bringing students to a better understanding of the world. For the past fifty years, there has been a retreat into specialization and disciplinary prerogatives. Universities need to determine the key elements of a learned society that must be imparted to all students. All students need to understand the rudiments of science, mathematics, language, culture, history, and philosophy. They need to know the key thinkers in each of the disciplines, and need to know where the frontiers of learning are in all subject areas. They need to be globally aware and internationally prepared. In terms of the education of the undergraduate, narrowness of focus can produce narrowness of mind. Universities must stand for comprehensive understanding, even if it means cutting back on some elements of disciplinary training.

Universities need to capitalize on administrative efficiencies through inter-institutional collaboration. There are some terrific examples already in existence. The Canadian Association of Research Libraries has revolutionized digital information-sharing. Universities collaborate on insurance, through a national shared insurance system, saving millions of dollars in annual premiums. The centralized Ontario and British Columbia application centres have cut costs dramatically in this increasingly important area. There are local examples, like the tri-university library consortium involving the University of Waterloo, the University of Guelph, and Wilfrid Laurier University. The collaboration between the University of New Brunswick (Fredericton), the University of New Brunswick (Saint John), and St. Thomas University in many respects is a model of collegiality, co-operation, and good sense. There are many more such opportunities, often lost behind institutional priorities.

Universities need to redefine their expectations of faculty members, as demonstrated through tenure, promotion, and merit processes. At present, there is a strong bias in favour of traditional models of academic engagement—scholarly articles, academic books, research grants, and conference papers. These are all fine activities and should be continued and rewarded. Academics do—and want to do—so much more, but they are worried that it will not "count" for professional purposes and might even be held against them. Academics who help draft a new law, support an advocacy group, tackle a pressing social problem, work with a community, explain scientific matters to children in school, or otherwise apply their scholarly knowledge and professional abilities in an appropriate manner should be recognized for doing so. Changing the main assessment measures in the university would radically and quickly transform the academy from an inward-looking, discipline-focused institution into an outward-looking, applied and engaged instrument for constructive change. Incentives matter, and rarely more intensely than in the university setting.

The academic community needs to elevate the scholarship of synthesis to the highest level of respect and credibility. The vast proliferation of academic writing has created a tsunami of information, analysis, and argumentation. Keeping up with the literature in the field is almost impossible or, to put it more accurately, is possible only by defining the field in increasingly narrow terms. The generalist, the scholar who can read through the material, make sense of it, find connections and dissonance, and bring order to the scholarly enterprise, is going to be a key figure in twenty-first century academia. Universities' need to recognize that the ability to synthesize learning—as equal to if not above the ability to conduct original research—is essential if we are to survive the massive wave of scholarly writing and to find the most important lessons and insights in the wealth of original studies.

Revolutionary change is in the offing in terms of course design—and universities should lead rather than resist the change. Courses are always seen as the domain of individuals, reflecting their insights and personality and remaining their intellectual property. That position is not tenable in the twenty-first century. Wiki architecture—providing scholars from around the world with the ability to contribute to the development of course material—will forever change the way we assemble course material and teach. Courses placed on the web and available for regular revision and editorial change will be available in multiple languages (thanks to rapidly improving web-based translation devices) and could be listened to by students (check out the vocal abilities of the latest Kindle e-book). Faculty from different backgrounds, cultures, experiences, and value systems can collaborative create, maintain, and adapt courses—and then retain their individuality through the actual delivery of the course online or in person. It really is time to get with the current generation.

Universities need to update and rationalize their governance systems. Current multi-level governance systems are slow, unwieldy, and subject to abuse. Faculty members spend far too much time in meetings, discussing matters that are really the purview of administrators, issues that in many cases committee members know and care nothing about. These structures cost money—particularly in faculty and administrative time—and they rarely capitalize fully on available technologies to assist with decision-making. Governance reform is essential. Certain key elements will have to be maintained: faculty control over academic programs, board control over financial and administrative matters. But streamlining, technology-based solutions, limitation of mandates, and other considerations must be taken into account. New financial realities will require greater attention to speed of decision-making, flexibility in resource allocations, the capacity to open and close programs more quickly, responsiveness to societal and economic trends, and a much higher level of innovation. Governance systems will have to be amended to respond to these realities.

Universities must stop trying and pretending to be alike. At the risk of repeating this fact once too often, we will reiterate one final time what is the essential reform that must come about in order to rationalize the post-secondary system: we must abandon the "Lake Wobegone" model, in which all places are above average, and all pretend to be high-quality research and teaching institutions. This pretense, which was never true and is becoming increasingly less so, is a recipe for mediocrity, decline, and ultimate disaster. Instead, different institutions should adopt different models, aiming for different markets and different goals. Canada supposedly celebrates diversity, and must do so in our post-secondary system, and the sooner the better.

These are tumultuous times for universities. The next decade will bring, in our opinion, more criticism, greater financial challenges, and more resistance from students, parents, employers, and government. The essence of a university—bright students studying with talented faculty members—is as exciting as it was when Canadian universities were first created. Universities are aggregations of very bright people—students, faculty, staff, and administrators. Properly mobilized, they can help this country develop a university system that is ready for the challenges of the twenty-first century. At present, universities are in a defensive posture, intent on preserving their andate and many benefits, more demanding of society than responsive to it. There is unrest in the country about this laudable but expensive, valuable but conservative, exciting and frustrating university system. It truly is time that universities, governments, and society at large rethink and debate the future of the Canadian university system.

Sources

A wealth of information on Canadian and foreign universities is available to anyone with access to a computer. All universities have websites, where information about enrolment size, courses offered, fees, calendars, and the like can be found. The Canadian Association of University Teachers, Statistics Canada, the Canadian Federation of Students, and provincial departments of post-secondary education are all good sources of information, as is the *Chronicle of Higher Education,* an American publication that publishes superb articles on post-secondary education that are relevant to Canada as well. The figures on participation rates for men and women in post-secondary education cited throughout this book come from Statistics Canada. Among the most useful sources for information on Canadian universities are the *Bulletin* of the Canadian Association of University Teachers (available on-line), *University Affairs,* and the *Rae Report* (a 2005 review of post-secondary education in Ontario chaired by former premier Bob Rae). The annual *Maclean's* university issue is invaluable, as is a similar annual report from the Toronto *Globe and Mail.*

Books worth reading on Canadian universities include Ian D. Clark, Greg Moran, Michael L. Skolnik, and David Trick, *Academic Transformation: Forces Reshaping Higher Education in Ontario* (Montreal: McGill-Queen's University Press, 2009); Robert Bothwell, David Bercuson, and J.L. Granatstein, *The Great Brain Robbery* (Toronto: McClelland and Stewart, 1984); Robert Bothwell, *Petrified Campus: The Crisis in Canada's Universities* (Toronto: Random House, 1998); James Cote and Anton L. Allahar, *Ivory Tower Blues: A University System in Crisis* (Toronto: University of Toronto Press, 2007); James L. Turk, ed., *Universities at Risk: How Politics, Special Interests and Corporatization Threaten Academic Integrity* (Toronto: Lorimer, 2008); Howard C. Clark, *Growth and Governance of Canadian Universities: An Insider's View* (Vancouver: UBC Press, 2003); Tom Pocklington and Allan Tupper, *No Place to Learn: Why Universities Aren't Working* (Vancouver: UBC Press, 2002); and Indhu Rajagopal, *Hidden Academics: Contract Faculty in Canadian Universities* (Toronto: University of Toronto Press, 2002).

There are far more books per capita on American universities than on Canadian ones. This abundance reflects the struggle there to get into the best universities and the equally intense battle to succeed academically in the less prestigious, open-entry campuses. The United States has a large number of the world's best and wealthiest universities, and a much larger number in financial difficulty, struggling to cope with the same student and faculty issues that we have described for Canada. A partial listing of recent books published in the past two years alone provides some indication of Americans' obsession with their universities: Jonathan R. Cole, *The Great American University: Its Rise to Preeminence, Its Indispensable National Role, Why It Must Be Protected*; Gaye Tuchman, *Wannabe U: Inside the Corporate University*; Derek Curtis Bok, *Universities in the Marketplace: The Commercialization of Higher Education*; Mark C. Taylor, *Crisis on Campus: A Bold Plan for Reforming Our Colleges and Universities*; Frank Donoghue, *The Last Professors: The Corporate University and the Fate of the Humanities*; Marc Bousquet and Cary Nelson, *How the University Works: Higher Education and the Low-Wage Nation*; Louis Menand, *The Marketplace of Ideas: Reform and Resistance in the American University*; Ben Wildavsky, *The Great Brain Race: How Global Universities Are Reshaping the World*; Holden Thorp and Buck Goldstein, *Engines of Innovation: The Entrepreneurial University in the Twenty-First Century*; David Horowitz, *Reforming Our Universities: The Campaign for an Academic Bill Of Rights*; William G. Bowen et al., *Crossing the Finish Line: Completing College at America's Public Universities*; Taylor Walsh and William G. Bowen, *Unlocking the Gates: How and Why Leading Universities Are Opening Up Access to Their Courses*.

Chapter 1. "The drop-out rate." Sometimes this means the number of first-year students who don't come back for a second year, and sometimes it means students who don't complete a degree. In 2006 Concordia University reported that only 54 per cent of its full-time students completed a degree in six years (*Vancouver Sun*, October 31, 2006). At the University of Windsor in 2010, 20 per cent of first-year students did not return for a second year (*CTV News* online, November 3, 2010; see also *Edmonton Journal*, November 21, 2007). The figure of 92 per cent comes from McGill Enrolment Services Admissions Profile, Fall 2009 Admissions, http://www.mcgill.ca/es/profile.

Chapter 2. A translation of the CLASSE manifesto is available at http://www.stopthehike.ca/2012/07/share-our-future-the-classe-manifesto/.

Chapter 4. Historical statistics on tuition fees and student debt levels are available online from Statistics Canada. Current fees are posted on each university's website.

Chapter 6. Macleans.ca on campus, February 26, 2008, has a discussion of the victory lap, with particularly interesting comments from students. See also Kelly

Pedro, "The Victory Lap," *London Free Press*, August 29, 2009 online. 45 per cent of Ontario students do not complete high school in four years. For the government's new policy, see "'Grade 13' sparks fears for disadvantaged students," *Hamilton Spectator*, April 10, 2012.

Chapter 7. The *McGill News Alumni Quarterly* for Fall 1998 has a good article on the admission process, written in the days when the cut-off rate was 80 per cent. On the UBC entering grade, see http://oncampus.macleans.ca/education/2010/07/08/your-grades-will-drop.

Chapter 9. See Paul Davidson, "University is Still the Surest Path to Prosperity," *Globe and Mail*, September 3, 2010. Figures on graduates working at jobs for which they are overqualified can be found at "Where do graduates end up doing unskilled work? And earning most?" *The Economist*, September 9, 2010.

Chapter 10. Figures for participation by age and gender are taken, here and elsewhere in this book, from Statistics Canada. Rick Miner's book is available on-line. The figures for the number of high school graduates in Ontario can be found at http://www.edu.gov.on.ca/eng/teachers/studentsuccess/CCL_SSE_Report.pdf, and the number from that province accepting offers of admission to universities at http://www.ouac.on.ca/statistics/ugrad-con-stats/ucon_september.

Chapter 12. Figures on people completing university, then going to college, can be found at accc.ca/ftp/pubs/studies/201104TransferabilityReport.pdf (see the chart on page 12).

Chapter 16. The Nova Scotia figures are from http://www.workitns.ca/documents/YouthDecisionSurveyReportfinal.pdf. For Skills Competences Canada, see http://www.newswire.ca/en/story/973515/vying-for-gold-in-the-trades-skills-canada-national-competition-to-take-top-talent-to-germany. National Graduates Survey, accc.ca/ftp/pubs/studies/201104TransferabilityReport.pdf (see the chart on page 12). The Estonian model, http://www.esu-online.org/blogs/blog/FINST/2012/06/29/Estonian-students-perception-of-Higher-Education-in-Scotland-amp-Estonia/.

Chapter 17. Rae's call for higher fees, along with increased grants, was not well received by the Canadian Federation of Students. See vivelecanada.ca, February 7, 2005.

Chapter 20. The Japanese are worried about declining student competence in math as well. See "Schools going back to the basics: 'Pressure-free education' gets blame for sliding exam scores," *Japan Times*, September 9, 2010. The 2009 study comes from the Organisation for Economic Co-operation and Development, and was reported in the *National Post*, December 7, 2010.

Chapter 25. Most Canadians donate at least something to charity: according to *CBC News*, 85 per cent made donations in 2006. The highest rate, 93 per cent, was in Newfoundland and Labrador; the lowest, 77 per cent, in British Columbia. But the bottom three-quarters of donors gave only 18 per cent of the donations (*CBC News* online, June 5, 2006).

Chapter 26. Statistics on foreign-born doctors in Canada are available from the Canadian Health Services Research Foundation. The figure of 22 per cent comes from an on-line article entitled "Mythbusters: Canadian doctors are leaving in droves for the United States" (http://www.cfhi-fcass.ca/Migrated/PDF/myth29_e. pdf). Ignatieff's proposal was announced in a press release on July 22, 2010.

Chapter 29. *Maclean's* (November 10, 2010) carried an article suggesting that American attempts to limit Asian enrolment at U.S. universities might divert the flow to Canada, making our universities "too Asian."

Chapter 32. In 2004, according to educationCanada.com, a teacher in B.C., the highest-paid jurisdiction in Canada, earned a maximum of $56,700 with four years of education, and $70,700 with six years. The top salary in that province now is about $90,000.

Chapter 33. The figure of 80 per cent of scientists is asserted by David Goodstein at http://www.its.caltech.edu/~dg/crunch_art.html.

Chapter 34. The lists of the councils' awards are available online.

Chapter 35. Shortage of spaces in the Greater Toronto Area: Ian D. Clark, "Challenges in University Financing and Accessibility in Ontario," presentation to the Faculty of Arts and Sciences Town Hall, University of Toronto, January 28, 2009.

Chapter 39. There's a debate on the merits of the three-year degree in *Maclean's*, February 27, 2012 (http://oncampus.macleans.ca/education/2012/02/27/ the-case-for-three-year-bachelor-degrees/).

Chapter 41. http://www.aucc.ca/wp-content/uploads/2012/09/quick-facts-back-to-school-2012.pdf; http://www.aucc.ca/media-room/news-and-commentary/ undergraduate-student-enrolment-surpasses-million-mark, 25 October 2011. AUCC gives different figures in different places; in another document they give the figure of 145,000; http://www.universityaffairs.ca/is-canada-producing-too-many-phds.aspx. Higher Education Quality Council of Ontario, http://www. heqco.ca/SiteCollectionDocuments/AtIssue7GradSummaryENG.pdf; http://www.

universityaffairs.ca/is-canada-producing-too-many-phds.aspx; http://www2.macleans.ca/2010/09/16/how-much-they-pay-for-it/.

Chapter 44. Figures for enrolment and degrees awarded by gender are available online from Statistics Canada. The historical statistic is from http://www.statcan.gc.ca/pub/11-516-x/sectionw/4147445-eng.htm#3. A table showing the number of women and men, full- and part-time, graduate and undergraduate from 2005 to 2009 can be found at http://www.statcan.gc.ca/daily-quotidien/100714/t100714a1-eng.htm.

Chapter 49. Oliver Goldsmith (1730–74), "The Deserted Village" (1770).

Chapter 70. There is an organization for English sessionals in Canada, affiliated with the Association of Canadian College and University Teachers of English. An article entitled "The Sessional Situation" posted on its website in June 2010 has a great deal of information about English sessional instructors in Canada: http://www.accute.ca/sessionalreport.html .

Chapter 75. The figure of 300 million was given in 2006 by Wu Qidi, a "senior Chinese education official," English.peopledaily.com.cn, March 27, 2006. This includes people who have studied it even briefly. Other sources give different figures: *Newsweek International* for August 20–27, 2007, gives a figure of 175 million.

Chapter 76. For default rates on student loans, see http://www.hrsdc.gc.ca/eng/learning/canada_student_loan/Publications/.annual_report/2004-2005/page08.shtml.

Chapter 78. Ed Dante, "The Shadow Scholar: The Man who Writes Your Students' Papers Tells His Story," *Chronicle of Higher Education*, November 12, 2010.

Chapter 81. Figures for fees tend to be elusive and hard to compare. The figure for Concordia is for tuition, but there are other compulsory per-credit fees—Student Service, Recreation & Athletics, Technology Infrastructure, and Copyright and Administrative fees. A more realistic figure is about $3,400 for the Montreal student, and $7,500 for the one from New Brunswick. The figures are available on the web from the individual universities. Statistics Canada reported that Quebec had the third-lowest university participation rate in Canada, while the president of McGill said it was the second lowest (Professor Heather Munroe-Blum, "Universities and the future of Quebec: Comme les deux doigts de la main," Speech to the Canadian Club of Montreal, June 14, 2010).

Chapter 82. The percentage of students becoming Ontario Scholars is from Alan Slavin, "Has Ontario taught its high-school students not to think?", *University*

Affairs, September 10, 2007.

Chapter 84. *University World News*, April 12, 2009, quotes official Chinese sources on graduate unemployment. Figures for the number of Chinese universities and university students vary according to source. The figure of eight million students comes from Wang Huiyao, Director General of the Centre for Globalization in Beijing and Vice-chair of the China Talent Research Society under the Ministry of Human Resources, quoted in Yojana Sharma, "China: Ambitious 'innovation society' plan," *University World News*, November 15, 2010, available online. Figures for the number of Canadians with degrees come from *1961: Census of Canada* (1963), Table 102, and subsequent censuses.

Chapter 86. David Bercuson, Robert Bothwell, and J.L. Granatstein, *The Great Brain Robbery* (Toronto: McClelland and Stewart, 1984).

Chapter 92. Figures from Statistics Canada. The numbers vary considerably from year to year. Spending in Canada, according to the Canadian Bureau for International Education, http://www.cbie-bcei.ca/?page_id=1233.

Chapter 93. Information on the Saskatchewan plan is available on-line at http://www.aeei.gov.sk.ca/grp.

Chapter 96. On working-class university participation, see Richard E. Mueller, *Access and Persistence of Students from Low-Income Backgrounds in Canadian Post-Secondary Education: A Review of the Literature*, MESA Project Research Paper (Toronto: Educational Policy Institute, 2008).

Chapter 97. Roger Martin has written and been interviewed extensively on business topics. A sample list of his work is available at http://www.rotman.utoronto.ca/FacultyAndResearch/Faculty/DeanRogerMartin/ArticlesByTheDean.aspx, and Marc Frenette, *Why Are Youth from Lower-income Families Less Likely to Attend University? Evidence from Academic Abilities, Parental Influences, and Financial Constraints*, StatsCan, http://www.statcan.gc.ca/pub/11f0019m/11f0019m2007295-eng.htm.

Chapter 100. On rankings, see *Maclean's*, http://oncampus.macleans.ca/education/2012/08/16/twenty-two-canadian-universities-in-new-ranking/, August 16, 2012.